HOW TO
Love
TEACHING
Again

HOW TO
Love
TEACHING
Again

· ·

WORK SMARTER, BEAT BURNOUT,

AND WATCH YOUR STUDENTS THRIVE

· ·

JAMIE SEARS

PORTFOLIO · PENGUIN

Portfolio/Penguin
An imprint of Penguin Random House LLC
penguinrandomhouse.com

Most Penguin Random House books are available at a discount when purchased in quantity for sales
promotions or corporate use. Special editions, which include personalized covers, excerpts, and corporate
imprints, can be created when purchased in large quantities. For more information, please call (212) 572-2232
or e-mail specialmarkets@penguinrandomhouse.com. Your local bookstore can also assist with
discounted bulk purchases using the Penguin Random House corporate Business-to-Business program.
For assistance in locating a participating retailer, e-mail B2B@penguinrandomhouse.com.

Library of Congress Cataloging-in-Publication Data

Names: Sears, Jamie, author.
Title: How to love teaching again : work smarter, beat burnout,
and watch your students thrive / Jamie Sears.
Description: New York : Portfolio/Penguin, [2023]
Identifiers: LCCN 2022041622 (print) | LCCN 2022041623 (ebook) |
ISBN 9780593539736 (paperback) | ISBN 9780593539743 (ebook)
Subjects: LCSH: Teacher effectiveness. | Teachers—Job stress—Prevention. |
Time management. | Teachers—Mental health.
Classification: LCC LB1025.3 .S3973 2023 (print) | LCC LB1025.3 (ebook) |
DDC 371.102—dc23/eng/20221123
LC record available at https://lccn.loc.gov/2022041622
LC ebook record available at https://lccn.loc.gov/2022041623

Printed in the United States of America
4th Printing

BOOK DESIGN BY ALISSA ROSE THEODOR

For the Not So Wimpy Teacher community

Thank you for your strength, your creativity, and your heart. You deserve so much more than a book, but my publisher refused to add cash bonuses to every copy.

CONTENTS

· · · · · · · · · · · · ·

HOW TO
Love
TEACHING
Again

INTRODUCTION

· · · · · · · · · · · · · · · · · · ·

 never wanted to be a teacher.

Lots of my childhood friends dreamed of becoming teachers, but I did not. Isn't it crazy that sometimes in life you end up wanting that thing you thought you would never want? Yeah, that happened to me.

When I finally became a teacher, I knew it would be difficult to balance work and family. I knew I wouldn't be making the big bucks.

But no one told me I would work sixty-plus hours per week.

I had no idea I would be buying and creating my own curriculum.

I didn't realize I would be paying for my own books and classroom furniture.

I had this ridiculous idea that students would be bringing me apples and parents would be sending glowing notes of appreciation. I thought I would have the tools I needed to teach and that I would go home every day at four o'clock.

Imagine my surprise when I was hired one week before school started and walked into an empty room. I remember asking the teacher down the hall what she was going to do with her students on the first day. She offered to give me a copy of her activities and I asked, "Where do I get paper to make copies for my students?" She laughed a little and informed me that I would need to buy my own paper.

And that was just the beginning. Before I stepped into the classroom, I did not understand standards and testing. I did not expect to be handed a list of more than sixty standards and have to twist everything I taught to what was on the list. Not to mention how stressful the tests were for the kids. Back when I was in school, I assumed the standardized tests were measuring us as students because after taking them we received reports on our individual performance.

But after I became a teacher, I realized that the tests were about *me* and *my* performance. How much I got paid was based on the tests, but the results didn't take student growth into consideration. A kid could come into my third-grade classroom at a first-grade reading level, do good work, and level up to second grade but still "fail" the third-grade test. This is frustrating to me as a teacher, and that result gives kids an incorrect impression of how smart and capable they are. It's not a fair system for anyone.

If your district is like mine, your school and district need to hit certain measures on the tests in order to get full funding from the state. If your kids do poorly on the tests, the school might face budget cuts and mandatory terminations, and you might lose your job. At first, I didn't really understand why there was so much pressure on tests compared to when I was growing up, but within a year of teaching, I understood it a lot better.

The whole system is pressurized because of the performance demands placed on districts by the state education systems, which force administrators to penalize teachers for poor performance. This ultimately transfers down to the kids, who feel like every test is make-or-break even if that's not articulated to them specifically. Not to mention that as a teacher, it's heartbreaking to watch a kiddo who's worked so hard all year to learn and grow do poorly because the test sucks.

Okay, enough complaining. I need to tell you something. The situations I described are real. The stress, the trauma, the drama . . . all real. And it can bring teachers like us to our breaking point. Daily. And maybe, maybe, make us consider quitting.

Teaching is hard.

If you're struggling, that's not because you're meant to do something else.

In fact, I know that you were *meant* to be a teacher. An amazing teacher, in fact. And with a little help, you can do hard things.

How do I know this?

Because I am just like you.

And I am the person who least expected to become a teacher.

Until I fell in love with teaching.

I am about to tell you something that might ruin our friendship before we even get to the point that you send me a friend request on Facebook. It's going to sound terrible, but please hear me out.

The truth is—and this is going to sound awful—I never wanted to be a teacher because I didn't like kids. Not one bit.

Don't get me wrong—I loved school. My cousin and I would play pretend school in my grandma's attic. Growing up, I had teachers who were inspiring.

Many of my family members were teachers.

But I wanted nothing to do with being a real teacher.

I did not grow up in a house full of kids. I have only one sibling and he is just one year younger than me. When all my friends were babysitting, I stayed home and read The Baby-Sitters Club. I met my husband, Scott, when we were in high school. One of the first things I said to him was, "I am never having kids. Never." He nearly broke up with me.

So how did I end up a mother of five standing in front of twenty-four third graders I loved fiercely?

It began during my sophomore year of college, when I decided it was time to get serious and work toward a "fancy" career. I studied political science and loved it so much that I talked myself into going to law school and becoming a bigwig lobbyist in Washington, DC.

I worked hard. I received almost all As and had a full load of classes each semester while working. I had the amazing opportunity to intern at the Arizona State Senate and then have a paper published in an academic journal on criminology. I graduated summa cum laude with honors and was accepted into a master's program for criminal justice. Everything was on track for my fancy job.

And then everything came to a crashing halt.

(Because that's what usually happens when you feel that everything is under control.)

I remember the day perfectly. Scott and I were newlyweds, and it was just a week after college graduation. We were cuddled on a pink couch that we got secondhand from a hotel and watching a show on TLC. The show was called *A Baby Story*, and it chronicled the pregnancy of a couple. Smack-dab in the middle of the show, I just had a feeling. It's the feeling you just can't describe or explain. I saw the baby on TV and my brain asked me something crazy.

"Are you pregnant?"

I ran into the bathroom and immediately took a test. The result was positive.

Scott and I did not believe it. He had recently had a checkup where the doctor had actually declared that I would never be able to conceive with Scott. Which had been fine with me—since I hated kids.

Now the girl who never wanted kids was having her own kid.

To say I was terrified would be a complete understatement. But strangely, I was also over-the-moon excited. The moment you know a baby is growing inside you, your heart completely changes. You love that baby with all your soul. I might not have planned to have a child, but in that moment everything changed and I decided I would be the best mother ever.

I spent the rest of the summer puking.

Morning sickness is a complete lie. I was sick every moment of the day.

In August, I had to make a huge decision. I was due to start my graduate program. But how could I sit through the classes and do the studying when I couldn't be more than ten feet from a toilet at all times? With a heavy heart, I withdrew from school.

When my son, Kyler, was born, I loved him more than I thought possible. I couldn't sleep at night because I was petrified that he would suddenly stop breathing. Once I got the hang of things, I thought about going back to school. But at the time, I was already rushing home from work every day so that I could give him a bath and read my favorite picture books to him. He was the center of our world.

And I had become a whole new person, the kind who actually loved kids.

Before I even had time to consider returning to school, when Kyler was just eleven months old, I found out I was pregnant again. That pregnancy was also difficult. The sickness was so bad that I landed myself in the hospital several times. Despite being pregnant, I was losing a dangerous amount of weight. After I was released from the hospital, an at-home nurse visited me regularly to administer IV fluids.

I was so excited for my twenty-week ultrasound. I just couldn't wait to find out the gender. I remember the tech asking me if this was our first ultrasound; I said it was. What she said next completely changed the course of my life.

"So you don't know that you are having twins?"

My response? "I have to pee."

For the next several weeks, I was an emotional mess—on a rollercoaster of emotions. Was I even capable of taking care of three kids? How would we fit all these babies in our two-bedroom apartment? How could I continue working?

The last fear was the kicker. I loved my job. At that point, I was working as a lobbyist at the Arizona Supreme Court. That job might sound fancy, but the pay wasn't great. It would cost us almost as much as I earned just to get daycare for three babies. It made no sense for me to continue working. So I quit.

It was hard to say goodbye to my job, but I was so darn busy that I didn't have time to think too much about it. Just three months after our twin girls were born, I found myself pregnant once again. I spent the next seven years changing diapers, attending playdates, and running millions of loads of laundry. Being a stay-at-home mom was a privilege and an honor, but I felt like something was missing.

I daydreamed about having a job outside of the home like my husband.

I felt guilty about those daydreams, so I kept them to myself for quite some time. While I was at home by myself, I quietly did some research. Since I had four babies and Scott was working at night while going to school during the day, I knew I couldn't do a traditional graduate degree program. I would need to do something that was completely online. When I was looking in 2007, there weren't very many graduate degrees that could be done online. In fact, the only one I could find that would be doable under my circumstances was a certificate in education.

I was instantly drawn to the program. I loved spending time with my kids all day—and this meant I could do it for a living. I could be a high school government teacher! It's not exactly like being a lobbyist, but it does include my love for politics. With Scott's support, I decided to go for it.

It was official: I was falling in love with teaching.

I finally got up the nerve to post about my big decision on Facebook. This was back in the day when Facebook was pretty new and there wasn't really a whole lot of etiquette about what to say and what not to say in the comments. My status was something like . . .

"Jamie Sears is . . . going back to school to become a teacher!"

Among all the congratulations and well wishes from family, one comment—from my cousin—stood out.

"You can't be a great teacher and a great mom. You'll suck at one of them."

That comment changed how I felt entirely. I was crushed. I was angry. I was scared.

I was hurt because my cousin—who was also my childhood best friend and my playmate in pretend school—didn't believe that I would be a good teacher. And at the time, I trusted her opinion. She was a successful middle school teacher. She didn't have any kids and prided herself on working every moment of every day for her students. I felt insulted and hurt that instead of offering me congratulations like everybody else, she criticized me. But I could deal with that.

What was tough was the fear in the back of my mind that she could be right.

Maybe it *was* impossible to be an exceptional mother and a great teacher. Perhaps I was being selfish by going back to school and pursuing a job outside the home. Was I really giving up on my own children? What business did I have being responsible for twenty-five kids in a classroom when I was barely managing to keep my four children alive at home most days? That one comment brought out all the doubts I had felt about being a great mother since childhood. And it seriously made me question my decision to go back to school and become a teacher.

Thank goodness for my friends who were both moms and teachers.

These ladies rallied behind me. They believed in my ability when I didn't believe in myself. Each one shared stories about how to handle motherhood and teaching. That it's possible to balance your needs and your family's needs. My friends continuously reminded me that you don't have to choose between family and a career.

You can have both and be amazing at both. And gradually I began to believe that was true for me too.

I already knew I was a hard worker. I started to feel like if anyone could be a kickass teacher and a great mom, I could.

So I started to do something that, at the time, felt crazy. I started taking education courses online while my babies were napping. It took three years, but every nap got me closer to my teaching certificate. That's how I ended up standing as a student teacher in front of thirty high school students who were not interested in civics. And later, once I was certified, twenty-four third graders I loved fiercely.

I was set on living a life that didn't include children, but thank goodness God had other plans for me. After having my own children, I could not imagine working with adults. All I wanted to do was talk to kids about their third-favorite reindeer. (Prancer, obviously.) I didn't want to read law textbooks because *The World According to Humphrey* was so much more fun. I became the best version of myself while eating PB&J with a group of eight-year-olds in miniature plastic chairs.

Prior to becoming a teacher, I took everything super seriously. I had the idea that I was going to be a super-duper successful big shot because achieving my goals had always come easily to me. I was *that* kid who got As in every class. I felt like everything I was doing in life was leading to one big thing—maybe being a Supreme Court justice or even the first female president of the United States. So it was funny when I decided to become a teacher because I had never thought that was particularly important or impressive. That's one of the many things I had wrong about teaching.

In the first week of teaching, I realized how big a deal I was going to be for my students. How much of an impact I could have on their lives. I realized that in addition to teaching reading and math, I'm teaching them to be good people. To be kind with others. To share, to collaborate, to work together and play together too.

To believe in themselves. I keep them safe, whether that's on the playground or after school or in an emergency. I am going to make them smile and laugh today—even the ones who have no reason to do that at home.

Ultimately, I realized teaching gives us a unique opportunity to make a difference that has nothing to do with multiplication or vocabulary. And despite growing up with teachers in my family, I had no idea what the job was really about until I was in the classroom myself. When I was teaching, I had students whose parents were in prison. I had to tell one child that his parents were getting divorced. One of my students lost a parent while he was in my classroom. Having that role and influence in a kid's life is monumental—and something no online course can prepare you for.

Once I became a teacher, I was humbled. It might not have been what I intended, but it was the role I was born to fill.

However, just because I was meant to be a teacher doesn't mean that teaching was easy for me. As it is for most of us, teaching was hard as heck for me. It's not your fault that there's not a lot of flexibility in the role of teacher. That you get surprised by a new curriculum, or that administrators spring some new rubric or system for grading on you in the prep period immediately before school starts. Or that your summers "off" are spent figuring out lesson plans and that your entire spring is eaten up by test prep and not actually teaching what kids need to know for the next grade. When I was a teacher, I spent so many nights sitting at my small kitchen table ugly crying to my husband.

I would say things like:

"Why am I so terrible at this?"

"The parents hate me."

"The kids don't listen."

"I never get everything done, even though I work all the time."

"I am so tired and frustrated."

"What's wrong with me?"

Have you been there? I don't mean my kitchen table (because that would be a little creepy). Have you been at your breaking point? Have you been to that dark place where you start to question whether teaching was a terrible mistake?

If so, you are not alone. I have been there—and I am writing this book for you.

For you and the thousands of other teachers who feel burned out as well.

That's right, you are not alone! Schools across our country hire tens of thousands of teachers each year just to replace those who leave the profession. This is a huge problem. Colleges and universities cannot train teachers fast enough to fill the vacant positions. Schools are hiring substitutes and uncertified teachers. Classroom sizes are growing.

More important, students are missing out. There are students who need to learn exactly how and what those teachers taught before they got burned out and left the profession.

But here's the truth: as teachers, we are experts at learning to solve problems.

There might not be a rubric to fix education, but I have some ideas—and I'm sure you do too—on where to start. We could and should start paying teachers better. We could start funding the curriculum, tools, and technology that teachers need for their classroom. We could rethink standardized testing that unfairly labels students and schools.

I will fight for all these things using my voice and my vote. But the reality is that none of these changes will come quickly and so this doesn't help *you*, the teacher who is exhausted and burned out now. Even though we have just met, I already love you and your heart for teaching children. I am not going to leave you hanging.

I started my business, Not So Wimpy Teacher, as a side hustle so I could earn more money and spend it on my classroom. By providing teachers with what they need to succeed both inside and outside of school, the business has grown to be a multimillion dollar company. But I have not forgotten my teacher days and how I went from feeling burned out to #blessed as a third-grade teacher. What's more, I am able to connect with thousands of teachers and design tools and strategies that help them work smarter and beat burnout.

In the pages that follow, you will find dozens of different strategies that helped me fall and stay in love with teaching, even when it was ridiculously hard. These are the lessons that I learned when I found myself crying at the kitchen table. When I felt wimpy, these strategies were the only thing that kept me from quitting.

I promise that I am sharing real tactics that you can start to use tomorrow.

These techniques and advice aren't just fluff that looks good on paper but will never work in a real classroom. I don't do fluff. In these pages, you're going to find real advice. But you'll also find lots and lots of stories. I can't help myself. Not only do I love to read and write, but I know firsthand how strategies can be hard to re-member, but stories are hard to forget.

Not So Wimpy Teacher has a handful of free Facebook groups for elementary school teachers. And something I see nearly every day in our members' posts is the idea my cousin had: that you have to choose between being a good parent and being a good teacher. That a single role in our life—teacher, mother, wife—needs to be more important or take up more time.

A lot of teachers believe that more hours means better teaching. But that's in-correct. The truth is, you can be a good teacher no matter how much time you spend grading or lesson planning.

Think about it for a second. Being "good" at something isn't about the *quantity* of time you spend but rather the *quality.* That's true for lots of things in life—being a student, for example, but also being a spouse. Or being a friend, a sibling, a mom, or a dad. How effective and supportive we are in those roles is not determined by how many hours we spend. Instead, our impact is decided by what we do with the time we have. When we're studying, are we really paying attention or watching TV? On date night, are we actually listening to what our loved one is saying? Or are we distracted and tuned out? When we're spending time with family and friends, are we enjoying the moment or wondering when we'll be able to get back to our grading?

The same truth applies to teaching. When we're lesson planning, are we concentrating on that task or taking lots of peeks at social media? I bet you can see where I'm going with this. Somewhere along the way, educators decided that the Teacher of the Year award goes to whoever's car is the last in the lot. But that's a bunch of bullcrap that has nothing to do with being a quality teacher. In fact, I would argue that it's the least efficient teacher who leaves school last—not the best.

It's my mission with this book to help you fall in love with teaching again. To start, I'm going to walk you through a fun exercise where you get to define—*for yourself*—the kind of teacher you want to be. And yes, that's a good teacher. *A great teacher*, actually. *An exceptional teacher.* The kind who gets letters from her students in the mail years or even decades down the road, thanking her for the difference she made in their lives. I wanted to be that teacher and I know you do too.

So: if you're ready to get started, I'm ready to help you.

Let's fall in love with teaching, shall we?

· · · · · · · · · · · · · · · ·

CHAPTER ONE

The Standards for Being a Great Teacher

hen I was a student teacher, I taught twelfth-grade government. Or so I thought.

I had 150 students in total. Every time I gave an exam, one-fourth would fail. As a former lobbyist and always perfectionist, I was dumbfounded. I had given my students solid lessons, great notes, and a super resourceful study guide.

But thirty-seven kids *still* flunked every unit test I gave. As I made red mark after red mark, I beat myself up about what a terrible student teacher I was and how no school would ever hire me. Yup, I am pretty dramatic. The teacher who was mentoring me at the time—one of my favorite teachers from high school—told me to be patient with myself. He didn't seem worried in the least. And you know what?

Every single one of those 150 students passed the course and graduated. Despite failing my unit tests. Many went to college and I hope all of them learned enough in my class to understand the importance of voting. (Please vote.)

But what I learned through that experience is that my classroom—and yours—isn't the last place your students will learn. About math, English, social studies, government, and life. Our educational journey is long. There are tough times for every student along the way. What I want you to realize and remember is that your classroom is *not* the final destination. You are just one stop on every student's educational journey. The kids in your class get to make other stops along the way. Each stop—from first grade to sixth grade to twelfth grade and beyond—is another opportunity for a new adventure and lessons learned.

So—deep breath here—it is perfectly okay if every student does not meet and exceed each testing standard while in your classroom. Yup, I said it. Every kid isn't the same. An entire class of kids can't all learn and grow at the same pace, and therefore, every student won't end at the same place at the end of this school year. Those who wrote the standards might not know this, but you and I are smart cookies. We know with certainty that every kid in our classroom, regardless of current grade—or reading!—level, will have a different experience with their education.

We're taught that students' overall education is the goal when we learn to teach, but in practice it's easy to forget and lose perspective. It can be so tempting to base our self-worth as teachers on student test scores. A few kids don't pass their math-facts test and suddenly you are spiraling in despair about what a terrible teacher you are.

If you are doing this right now, take a breath. You are not alone. I did it too. Teachers face so much pressure for their students to perform on tests when, really, standardized testing is just one data point and can be irrelevant to the quality of teaching that is actually happening in the classroom.

You love your students. You want them to succeed. But *their* success is not the definition of being a great teacher. Think back to your favorite teacher from school. Did you like them because you always got As on their tests? I doubt that's the reason you still fondly think of them as a great teacher. Instead, I bet you loved that teacher because of how they made you feel, how they spoke to you, what they believed or noticed about you that others didn't.

My mentor teacher when I was student teaching was actually *my* government teacher in high school. Mr. Craig was one of my all-time favorite teachers because he talked to me like I was brilliant. He treated me like an adult and believed I was capable of succeeding at hard things. That's why my definition of a great teacher is listening to, believing in, and pushing your students. It's not about having the best test scores in your district.

I wanted to be a great teacher. I knew that from the moment I made it Facebook official that I was going back to school to become a teacher. However, even though I knew in my heart that I could be a great teacher, I had my doubts. I kept hearing my cousin's words in my head. "You can't be a great teacher and a great mom. You'll suck at one of them." I just had to prove her wrong, even if I didn't know quite how to make it happen.

When teachers in the Not So Wimpy Teacher

> When I was writing this book, I asked my Facebook community of teachers to share their stories. Throughout the book, you'll see their words in these handy boxes.

> "I reviewed for success! I would have my students try an old skill from the beginning of the school year. We would be able to see how much easier those skills were. The message: tests are designed to see what you have already learned!"   **—Elsa H.**

Facebook groups post about feeling like bad teachers, it reminds me of marshmallows. That seems weird, right? But I promise—it'll make sense after I share a story. Before I got married, my mom threw me a bridal shower and invited lots of her friends. None of my friends came because we were all broke college students at the time, and it was hard enough for us to scrounge up gas money, much less gravy boats and china. Driving to my mom's house on the day of the shower, I felt grateful for the generosity of my mom and her friends, and excited for the actual party. And it was fabulous. Except for the games.

There was one game in particular I will never forget. Prior to my bridal shower, my mom asked Scott some questions about himself. Then, at the bridal shower, she asked me the same questions. If I got the question right, we went on to the next question. But if I got it wrong, I had to put a *giant* marshmallow in my mouth. I wasn't allowed to chew it or swallow it. I just had to keep it in my mouth until the end of the game.

My mom started asking questions, and it became apparent very quickly that I had been set up. To this day I don't know if it was my mom, or Scott, or if they were in on it together . . . but *I got every question wrong*. Even the ones I knew for sure—like what size shoes Scott wore. I mean, I bought his shoes! I was sure I had the right answer. But another marshmallow was added to my mouth.

It went on and on like this. I knew all the answers. But every answer Scott had given was inaccurate. It didn't matter, though, because according to the rules of the game I had to keep adding marshmallows to my mouth while all her friends laughed hysterically. I ended up with a mouth full of massive marshmallows. It was awful. And it was hard for me to breathe. By the end of the game, I was gagging and couldn't even answer the questions because of the marshmallows.

To this day I can't even think about marshmallows without feeling nauseated.

Teaching is a lot like having a mouth full of marshmallows. When you first graduate from college, you have just one marshmallow. It's sweet and delicious. You love it so much. You are so excited about your career path and spend lots of time dreaming about the lives you will impact in your super-fun, totally cute classroom.

Then you get your first job and another marshmallow is added. You're excited, but also nervous. You have so many decisions to make. What should you buy? How should you set up your classroom? Should you have themes? Next, there are professional development and staff meetings on your schedule. Marshmallows are now being added two at a time. You have to learn standards, and a new curriculum is thrown at you. It's starting to get hard to breathe. Every day, more is added to your load.

And that analogy is true for all teachers. Seasoned teachers come to school with a mouth full of marshmallows but continue to try to squeeze in more than can comfortably fit. Teaching becomes like shoving more marshmallows into your mouth than you can hold without gagging. You're being asked to join committees and clubs and to volunteer to coach sports teams. As soon as you figure the curriculum out, a new one is introduced. The pressure is always on to come up with more engaging and differentiated ways to teach the lessons. And just when you think you can't fit one more marshmallow in, you are assigned a student teacher and asked to mentor them. Does that sound about right?

The truth is that there is a tremendous cost to letting those marshmallows pile up. One Not So Wimpy Teacher, Alyse, had a powerful wake-up moment. Alyse used to work all weekend prepping for the week. One Saturday, her husband stood between her and her computer and said, with tears, "I miss my wife." She didn't realize how bad things had gotten. When she decided to reserve weekends for family, she learned she was doing too much for school and not enough for home. And guess what? Even though she wasn't working around the clock for her students, they still loved her.

As teachers, most of us know we are gagging and struggling to breathe. So why do we keep adding more to our plate? It's simple. We do it because we want to be great teachers for our students. It's all we have ever wanted and the reason we chose this career path. But does all that overwhelm, all those marshmallows, make for a great teacher? And what *is* a great teacher, anyway?

When I first started teaching, I didn't really know what a great teacher was. I was watching the other teachers around me and looking to them for guidance. I started to follow teachers on social media. They became my mentors. Without even realizing it, I had defined in my mind what being a good teacher meant.

And like a lot of the people I talk to online—and maybe you too—I couldn't ever live up to the image I had crafted in my mind because I believed three huge myths about being a good teacher. After working with tens of thousands of teachers, I now know that most teachers have believed at least one of these myths at some point in their career—and have felt like they were never good enough as a result.

Myth #1 • GOOD TEACHERS WORK LONG HOURS.

The good teacher arrives at school early and is the first in line at the copy machine.

Their car is the last in the parking lot at night.

It's dark by the time they leave.

When they leave school, the good teacher has the largest bag and it is always stuffed full with papers to grade and lesson plans to complete.

The good teacher spends a good chunk of their weekend preparing amazing lessons for the following week.

The good teacher almost always drops by the school on their day off.

Good teachers are willing to put in any number of hours necessary to help their students succeed. That's just what good teachers do.

The teachers I admired the most during my first years on the job always beat me to school in the morning. Most took so much work home that a bag wouldn't do. Instead, the teachers I was trying to emulate had carts with wheels to drag work home with them. These teachers were always signing up to lead committees, coach teams, sit in on interviews, and volunteer for parent-teacher-night activities.

> "My kiddos have been coming to my classroom since they were only weeks old. My oldest son stays one hour before and after school hours with me so I can get stuff done. I still bring things home after that. My husband says he can be considered an honorary teacher with all the crafting I make him do. He has done more tracing and cutting than he cares to admit."   —Andrea P.

I've heard horror stories about what teachers do in order to get all their work done. One member of our Not So Wimpy Teacher Facebook group admitted to sleeping in her classroom a couple nights a week. Another teacher used to stay at school so late that she had to use the fire escape to leave because otherwise she would set off the alarm.

Like a lot of my fellow teachers, I too started to believe that if I wanted success in the classroom, I was going to have to put in significantly more hours. If you've ever thought, "I need to find a way to sleep less and work more," then you may believe the myth that good teachers have to work long hours and dedicate their whole lives to their jobs, like I did.

But here's the thing—can you think of a teacher you know who gets great results in the classroom and has amazing relationships with their students but does not work on weekends?

I can. The teacher who taught next door to me used to leave every day at her contracted time (or even slightly before). She set boundaries for when parents could contact her. She didn't do a lot of over-the-top activities. She focused on building relationships with her students. She didn't grade everything. Yet her students experienced a lot of growth and parents loved her. Teachers like her prove that working on weekends isn't mandatory to be a great teacher.

Similarly, can you think of a teacher who works all hours but still struggles to make her lessons effective and meet the needs of her students?

I can—because she was in my classroom. (Spoiler alert: it was me!)

When I first started teaching, I was spending my time doing all the wrong things. I was creating brand-new center activities for every week, putting cute covers on all my binders, and printing free resources from Pinterest that I would never have time to use. I was working a lot of hours, but the tasks I chose to complete did not always help me or my students to be more successful.

But here's the truth.

You can be an amazing teacher and work a reasonable number of hours.

You can also work a ton of hours and not get the results you desire. In the end, what you do with your time matters more than the number of hours you work.

My point is, there is no relationship between good teachers and time spent teaching.

Myth #2 • IF YOU DO MORE, YOU'LL BE A GOOD TEACHER.

A good teacher is always bringing new and innovative activities to the classroom.

A good teacher does science projects and even art projects that involve paint *and* glitter.

Good teachers do full-on room transformations for math. Good teachers spread out a variety of perfectly appropriate books and allow kids to read the first chapters in an arrangement that looks super cute for reading. Good teachers always switch out their bulletin boards and create anchor charts with hand lettering that looks borderline professional. Good teachers have time to do social and emotional learning lessons as well as music appreciation.

I don't know about you, but the teachers I admired on social media were always doing something amazing in their classroom. Their lessons all looked picture-perfect and involved an elaborate amount of supplies. It seemed that they were always doing something new.

I started to believe that if I wanted to be a good teacher, I was going to have to ditch the traditional lessons and come up with something outlandish to excite my students. If you have ever felt like what you're doing isn't good enough and that you need to do more, then you may believe this myth, like I did.

I bet you know a teacher who is always trying some new fad in their classroom but really struggles to differentiate and meet the needs of their students. Maybe they have a fun classroom, but they're just slightly missing the learning targets.

Or maybe you see the opposite. Perhaps there's a teacher in your school or district who is fairly traditional but getting amazing results. These teachers may rely on textbooks and don't add a ton of bells and whistles to their lessons or their classroom. From the outside, these teachers seem happy and aren't stressing about keeping up with trends or others' standards. For example, there was a teacher at my school who always had very simple lessons. There weren't a lot of complicated games or heavily designed resources. I thought maybe her students would be bored. It turned out that parents were raving about her and begging the principal to put their kids in her classroom.

Clearly, you can add all kinds of fun to your classroom but still struggle to help your students make connections and understand key concepts. You can also have a teacher who does the bare basics, gets extraordinary results, and is the favorite teacher on campus.

These examples show that doing more isn't what makes a great teacher.

Myth #3 • GOOD TEACHERS HAVE STUDENTS WHO HAVE HIGH TEST SCORES.

Good teachers don't have to worry about a class full of students scoring poorly on their math test. Good teachers always meet and exceed the growth goals set by the administration for every subject. Good teachers offer such quality lessons all year that there's no need to spend time prepping for standardized tests.

After all, the students in a good teacher's classroom all pass the test with flying colors.

Okay—let's stop for a minute. Do you know the test scores of every other classroom in your school? I never actually did. I just decided that every other teacher's score must be amazing. I assumed that every student in all the classrooms—except mine, obviously!—was growing by leaps and bounds and that it was easy for good teachers to get great scores for standardized tests. If you've made the same assumptions, you're not alone.

I also thought that if I wanted to be a good teacher, I was going to have to teach and reteach each skill until my entire class had mastered every single standard. I would need to secretly bust my butt so that all my students would receive passing scores on the end-of-year testing. I also had to make that feat look easy, because obviously all of that would be a piece of cake if I was a good teacher.

Looking back—this was a bit crazy. If you can relate to stressing and losing sleep all year over test scores, then you understand what I was feeling. I would constantly think things like, "If I can just find a way to bring up test scores, then I'll finally be a good teacher."

Excuse my French, but I am calling malarkey with a big side of poppycock!

Can you think of a teacher you admire who does not get the test scores the school would like? There was a teacher at my school I loved to watch in her classroom. She had so much patience and the unique skill of helping students to keep trying even when their first attempts were inaccurate. Her students were so engaged in her lessons. One day she admitted that several of her students were not meeting the testing goals.

Do you know teachers who brag about their test scores, but every time you walk into their classroom it feels like a hot mess? I bet you do.

It's totally possible to be an effective, loved, and great teacher without the highest test scores in your school or district. That's because great test scores don't make you a great teacher.

If I were to tell you that in order to be a great teacher you must work long hours, take on more projects, and get the highest standardized test scores, you would probably tell me that I am crazy. Most of you would argue that there is so much more to being a great teacher than the cute bulletin boards and benchmark tests. And you would be right. You know that this definition of a great teacher is a myth.

But if you are being honest with yourself, even though you don't believe these statements to be true, you often show up and act as if you do believe them. Don't feel bad. You're in good company. I did it in the classroom and I do it in my personal life too. I don't believe that a good mom has to buy tons of toys for her kids. However, I still overbuy every Christmas, and then I become frustrated when we have to find space for all the new belongings. I don't believe in allowing children to spend too much time staring at screens. Yet all my teenagers have their own phones and spend most of their free time watching videos and Facetiming with friends. (I hope you're not judging me, but if you are . . . I understand!)

Let's talk about how we show up in the classroom.

I don't believe that good teachers work the longest hours, but I spent several weeks every summer decorating my classroom. I would drag four kids in with me and bribe them to sit quietly using a movie and Pop-Tarts.

I don't believe that in order to be a good teacher you have to do all the things. Still, I would spend a Saturday searching Pinterest for the perfect art project. Then I would drag all my kids to the craft store to search for the needed supplies.

You may have taken "all the things" to an even greater extreme. One Not So Wimpy Teacher, Gricelda, used to pay for her teaching assistant to come in on weekends—even though she couldn't afford it—and help her grade and prep for the following week.

I don't believe that high test scores are the mark of a good teacher. However, I always spent my spring break stressing about standardized testing. I would spend hours looking for new games and creating engaging test prep activities.

At the time, I would have told you straight to your face that I didn't believe any of those myths. But how I showed up nearly every day revealed that deep down, I did believe them. The very logical side of my brain knew those statements were ridiculous. But there was this tiny voice in my head that said, "Yeah, but . . ." And I would find myself, over and over, making decisions in the classroom that were not in alignment with what I know to be true. What about you?

If you are still showing up like you believe in those myths, I'm not judging you one bit. Keep reading because we are about to get very clear about what it means to be a good teacher and how we can show up every day in a way that aligns with that.

Many of us subscribe to a definition of success that doesn't work and is just plain wrong. Being a successful teacher is not based on the hours you work, Pinterest-worthy classroom decor, or standardized test scores. After all, if working all the time, being a near-professional crafter, and having my entire class ace every single test is what it means to be a good teacher, then my cousin is right. I can't juggle all these things and still be a sane person, a good mom, an attentive wife, and a go-to friend. And neither can you.

The reality is that we have been defining "good teacher" wrong all this time. Over the years, I tried and I tried to come up with a more accurate definition, but I kept hitting a roadblock. There wasn't one definition that seemed to hold true for every single teacher out there. That's when it hit me like a dozen kindergarteners on the playground: success is personal. And that means the definition of success must also be personal. Every teacher has to decide their own definition of success. You get to decide what it means to be a good teacher! My mind was blown when I finally had this realization. A huge weight was lifted from my shoulders because I realized that I no longer needed to try to be the teacher my neighbor was, or the teacher my cousin was.

So this is the part of the book where I, personally, would probably skip ahead to the next chapter. (Don't do that. Hear me out.)

You see, I love practical strategies. Give me some "how to" and I am in my glory.

That's part of the reason I love creating and selling resources on Teachers Pay Teachers. But defining success? I would probably call that a little woo-woo. I'm not the woo-woo kind of person. So if "creating your personal definition of success" sounds like fluff to you, I see you and I totally get it. But stop! Let me explain.

This book is full of strategies you are going to love.

But reading the entire book and trying to implement every strategy tomorrow would be a whole lot like me giving you a Costco-size bag of marshmallows. You can't fit all of those in your mouth, and similarly, trying to do every single strategy in this book all at once would be so overwhelming. It's important to prioritize the strategies that are going to make the biggest impact for you right now. The only way to prioritize is to have your own personalized definition of success.

When you have a clear vision of what it means for you to be a good teacher, you will know exactly which strategies need to be implemented right this moment and which ones can wait until you have some space. We aren't just reading this book and then putting it on a shelf to collect dust. We are taking action. So let's start by creating the most meaningful, non-woo-woo definition we possibly can.

Step 1 • WRITE DOWN ONE WORD OR PHRASE TO DESCRIBE THE KIND OF TEACHER YOU WANT TO BE.

When you were in college and dreaming about the teacher you would one day be, what did that look like?

Or, when you are excitedly planning to go back to school (hopefully after having a restful summer), what kind of teacher do you dream about being?

The good news is that this does not have to be the kind of teacher you are at this very moment, and you don't have to know right now how to be this teacher. So dream big! The catch is that you can choose only one word or phrase. We don't want our definition of success to be any more complex than it needs to be. Don't go trying to creatively sneak in a detailed list, because that just makes success harder to achieve in the long run. And who wants that? Not that dream-teacher version of you. That said, if it helps, you can brainstorm a list, but when you are done brain dumping, go back and circle the one word that really speaks to you.

I've included a list of possibilities just in case you are having trouble getting started. This is *not* a comprehensive list. Every teacher is going to have a very different definition of success, and it's so important that you pick the words that light *you* up. Don't choose the phrase you think your principal would want you to pick. This is all about you.

Patient

Innovative

Creative

Inclusive

Engaging

Organized

Positive

Happy

Life-changing

Inspiring

Relational

Relaxed

Effective

Efficient

Intentional

I could go on and on because there are so many incredible words that might describe the kind of teacher you want to be. Don't overthink it. Go with the word that stands out to you at this very moment. You are not marrying this word. I give you permission to change it later if you need to.

Step 2 • WRITE DOWN ONE WORD OR PHRASE TO DESCRIBE THE RESULTS YOU WANT TO ACHIEVE IN THE CLASSROOM.

This one is a little harder, right? Later, when you look back on this school year, what is one thing you want to be able to say you achieved in the classroom?

What about when you retire and you are looking back on your career?

What is one thing you want to be able to say confidently that you accomplished?

You will do a million things as a teacher. It would be so easy to create a laundry list of things you want to achieve. But you get to pick only one. This means you have to really ask yourself what you consider the most important achievement on the list. (I am taking a wild guess that the most important thing won't be to have the highest test scores at your school. Please tell me I'm right! Seriously. Go to my Instagram and send me a DM.)

Here are some ideas in case you are stuck. Do not feel like you have to pick something from my list. My feelings won't be hurt if you go rogue and create a phrase of your own.

Instilling a love for learning
Developing a student's growth mindset

Fostering student independence

Inspiring students to be risk-takers

Generating student confidence

Creating a student-led classroom

Providing a safe and inclusive environment to learn

Encouraging student curiosity

Step 3 • HOW MANY HOURS DO YOU WANT TO WORK PER WEEK?

This is where it gets really fun! So few people ask themselves this question. We tell ourselves it isn't up to us; we have to work as many hours as it takes to do the job. Wrong! The truth is that you will fill as many hours as you give yourself to work and it will never seem like enough. There will always be something else on the list that you will feel guilty about not completing.

Has this ever happened to you? You have a huge to-do list around the house and an entire day to complete the tasks. The first half of the day, you get almost nothing done. (In fact, I usually add more to the list over the course of the morning than I actually get to cross off.) Then you realize your spouse/children/mother will be home in thirty minutes. Suddenly you kick it into high gear. You are completing tasks in record time. You might not complete the list, but you definitely complete more in those last thirty minutes than you did earlier in the day. Can you relate?

If you have ten hours to work in a day, you will fill all ten hours. If you have only eight hours to work in a day, you will likely find that you can complete the same amount of work. In fact, a recent study at Stanford showed that productivity drops

> "I have pulled many all-nighters grading papers, while also having children who were athletes. I spent many hours in the car grading papers between games [and] during tournaments on the weekends. I've stayed so late at work the security alarm has automatically gone off. I am a seasoned teacher now so lesson plans are done on Thursday nights and a week ahead."
>
> **—Terri R.**

off a cliff when we work more than fifty hours a week.* And if you work seventy-plus hours like some teachers do . . . well, you're wasting fifteen hours of your life every week, because you're getting the same amount done that someone who puts in fifty-five-hour workweeks does.

I want to come back to the question: How many hours do you *want* to work? You don't have to have a plan for how you will fit everything into these hours yet. Heck, you don't even have to believe that it is possible. For now, I will believe enough in the possibility for both of us. You just have to want it. If you want it, I will show you how to make it happen in the next chapter. (But you still can't skip ahead yet, you rule breaker!)

Here is a good way to come up with this number:

How many hours are you contracted to work? (Make sure to look this up, because you have been working such long hours that it's likely you have forgotten the actual requirement.)

How many additional hours do you want to work each day in the classroom or at home? (The key word here is "want.")

---

*John Pencavel, "The Productivity of Working Hours," IZA Discussion Paper Series: IZA DP No. 8129 (April 2014), https://docs.iza.org/dp8129.pdf.

Step 4 • WHAT IS ONE THING YOU WOULD DO WITH THE TIME WHEN YOU ARE NOT WORKING?

I am taking a stab in the dark and making the assumption that you probably chose a number in step three that is less than the hours you are currently working. It's a pretty safe assumption since you are reading a book about recapturing your love for teaching. Finding your love for teaching and working fewer hours really go hand in hand. It's hard to love a career that feels all-encompassing and leaves little time for a personal life. You will love your job ten times more when you also love your time outside work.

When you have achieved success and you are working the number of hours you want to be working, what will you do with that extra time? Start dreaming! Dump all your ideas here. I would try to be specific. Instead of "spend time with my family," you might write "go on more family bike rides." By choosing what you want to spend your extra time doing, you are more likely to look for these opportunities all week. Over time, the things you do outside school will motivate you to make the most of your time *at* school. Knowing exactly what you want to do will also make it easier to know when you have achieved success.

When you have a good, solid list, circle the one activity you want the most. That's what we will start with.

You might easily fill the page with things you would like to do with your new free time. But you might be like me. I couldn't think of anything! I realized that I had gone so long without time that I no longer had hobbies or things that I looked forward to doing in my personal time. It was a scary revelation. Don't fret if you are in the same predicament. I found that it took me longer than I expected to complete this step. I spent a few days thinking up my list. I asked my mom, my best friend, and my husband for some ideas. They remember who I was before I became a teacher, and that helped. I was reminded of my old love for reading, stamping, and scrapbooking. I also realized that I have new loves for lunch with friends and hair blowouts. Soon I had a decent list!

These activities become your why. It's why you are making changes. It's why you work to be more productive during your work hours. It's why you want to fall back in love with teaching.

Step 5 • PUT YOUR ANSWERS TOGETHER TO CREATE YOUR DEFINITION OF SUCCESS.

You have done all the work!

Give your brain a kiss because it helped you brainstorm what is really important to you. All you need to do now is take your answers from steps one to four and place them in order in this sentence.

Success for me is being a/an _____ teacher who _____ while working only _____ hours per week so that I can _____.

Here is my definition of success (which does *not* need to be similar to your definition):

Success for me is being an innovative teacher who helps students fall in love with learning while working only forty hours per week so that I can spend my weekends playing make believe with Adalynn.

Read your definition at least three more times.

Does it make you giddy?

Is your brain saying things like, "Sounds great, but it's wishful thinking"?

If so, you are on the right track! This is success for you. But if the definition does not light you up like a package of brand-new Crayola crayons, then you might have some editing to do. Don't fret. This can be a draft version of your definition. You can keep coming back to it during the next few days. Go back to the four prompts and play with different words and phrases until you hit the nail on the head and feel super excited about your definition of success.

It's important to note that your definition of success will change. You may switch schools or grade levels and decide on new priorities. You will grow as an educator and have new ideas about the results you want in the classroom. You may decide to buy resources (including what's available on Not So Wimpy Teacher, made by yours truly) instead of creating everything yourself. Your family and friends may change and grow and cause you to change what you want to do with your personal time. I'm also quite confident that you are going to learn some amazing productivity hacks in this book, and some of you will want to change the number of hours you work. You are not married to this definition, or any definition that you create for yourself. When you feel that it no longer speaks to you, feel free to make edits. The important thing is that the definition is yours. You are no longer measuring your success based on what society, your admin, or your students' parents think that it should be. Success is personal. You're the only person who can write your definition of success.

I don't like busy work. I didn't like busy work as a student and I definitely didn't like it as a teacher. (I mean, who needs one more stack of papers to find a home for?) I want you to know that writing this definition was *not* busy work.

Your definition of success is going to help you prioritize and make decisions about how to use your time. For example, when you are considering staying late at school to add a new app to the class iPads, I want you to ask yourself, "Is this going to help me to get closer to my definition of success?"

If the answer is yes, then by all means get downloading! But if you are being really honest with yourself, and the answer is no, that does not mean your iPads will forever be filled with apps that were so last year. It just means you might not get that new game right away. And you can leave school without guilt.

If that's not enough and you still feel bad about not staying late, I want you to ask yourself a few more questions:

1. *Is there anyone who can help me complete this task?*

2. *Can this wait until I have some flex time or time during my scheduled work hours?*

3. *Can I let this go completely, knowing that it is not essential for my success or the success of my students?*

If you ask yourself these questions when you aren't tired and overwhelmed, you will be surprised at the solutions your brain will offer up.

Maybe you will realize that it isn't as important as you originally thought.

Or maybe you will ask a parent volunteer to come in and do the download one day while you are teaching. In any case, you won't automatically defer to the idea that you *have* to do it or you won't be a good or effective teacher.

· ·

If you have time to do only one thing
from this chapter, I want you to:

Define what "success" means to you.

Fill in the blank (my favorite kind of question on a quiz!):

Success for me is being a/an _____ teacher who _____ while working

only _____ hours per week so that I can _____.

· ·

The Not So Wimpy Way to Be a Good Teacher

1. Define your version of success as a teacher (pages 26-32).

2. When you are tempted to work more than the hours you want to work, ask yourself the key questions on page 34.

3. When everyone is freaking out about standardized tests, remind yourself that:

   - A test is just a snapshot of where a child is right now—and does not indicate future success.

   - Your value as a teacher is not determined by any test, ever.

   - Testing serves as one point of accountability for your district and isn't meant to be *everything* that will ever happen in your classroom.

   - You're not alone in how you feel.

CHAPTER TWO

Ditch Your To-Do List

hen I was teaching the rock cycle to my third graders, I had a brilliant idea.

I thought it would be a blast to do a *Magic School Bus* theme for the lesson. But—as you may have guessed—I am not one to go halfway when it comes to themes. I go all in.

I showed up to school in a homemade Ms. Frizzle costume.

It was an enormous blue dress hot glued with colorful pieces of fabric that looked like rocks and a huge volcano. I even went as far as to wear a red wig and attach an iguana to my shoulder.

I looked out of this world.

My students and I had a blast studying different types of rocks, making rocks from different foods, and watching *The Magic School Bus*. It was a super-fun day of learning.

At the end of the day, I checked my email and my stomach dropped.

I had totally forgotten about the Individualized Education Plan (IEP) meeting I had after school! (It must have slipped my mind while I was hot gluing my dress together.) There was no way I could miss or reschedule the meeting. Those meetings are so hard to schedule in the first place.

But . . . I didn't have a change of clothes.

I had no choice. I attended the meeting dressed in full Ms. Frizzle garb. There I was in a room with the director of special education, the speech pathologist, the school psychologist, and my student's mom and dad. I was the only one wearing a red wig and an iguana. I decided to play it cool and pretend like nothing was amiss. No one even asked about my outfit, but I'm guessing I was talked about at the dinner table that night.

On my way home, I had a serious headache. I wanted a soda. I thought, "Why not?" and went through the drive-through at Sonic. I saw the employee look at my outfit. I just smiled and thanked her for my drink.

I know what you're probably thinking: this girl needs to learn to plan ahead.

But what if I told you I had an elaborate plan for my entire week and month? That I had written a to-do list that should have had me covered for every hour of the day?

This is when I learned that to-do lists aren't foolproof.

I'm going to teach you something unexpected in this chapter—which is how to plan *without a to-do list*. I know! Crazy, right? But it's super effective. That said, I will warn you: no system is perfect. Even the best planners sometimes show up to a stuffy meeting wearing ridiculous costumes. It's just the reality of being a teacher!

If you are like me, you are a fan of lists. Most of the teachers I meet are.

It's time to take a big breath because I am about to suggest something wacka-doodle.

You don't need *any* to-do lists. In fact, as I'll show you, to-do lists only serve to make you busier, while minimizing the number of important tasks you complete. Go ahead and toss your to-do lists in the trash—or the recycling if you want to be responsible about it. Again, I know this might seem wackadoodle, but the truth is that every to-do list is really just a laundry list of things you *think* you need to complete.

Here is the real psychology of to-do lists: the list becomes so overwhelming that your brain decides there is no way that it can complete everything. That's when you end up using your plan time to gossip with your teacher bestie or you use your grading time to scroll through social media. (Of course these activities are perfectly fine if you are intentionally setting aside time for them. It becomes a problem when you were supposed to be grading papers and now you have to bring those papers home to grade during time that should be spent with family or friends.)

Your to-do list isn't a plan for action. Instead, it's an excuse to procrastinate or to set yourself up to fail. I actually didn't know this when I was a teacher. I learned the hard way when I was an overwhelmed, burned-out entrepreneur. A lengthy to-do list can cause us to feel frustrated and disappointed when we don't need to. That's because nothing is ever *really* done. As ambitious educators, we don't blame the million things on our to-do list. We blame ourselves.

Contrast your lengthy to-do list to a calendar, which is a list of things to do at a specific hour or within a defined window of time. We succeed with the calendar whenever we show up and do what we're supposed to do. When we follow the plan, we win—and get to celebrate! It's a perfect system for anyone with a get-the-gold-star mindset like me (or you). After all, teachers are already great at following calendars and schedules—you don't teach math during reading time, do you? Of course not!

Ready for a little laugh?

Most teachers have heard the excuse: "My dog ate my homework."

(I love when students bring the leftover pieces as evidence!)

Watch out for your calendar, because once I ended up in tears after discovering that my dog ate my calendar. After doing my Sunday-night planning, I left the calendar on the kitchen counter. Apparently, I left it too close to the edge, and Penny was able to grab it. I have no idea why she wanted to take a bite out of every darn page. It's not like it was coated in bacon juice. Nonetheless, she ate it. I was so sad to see my beautiful calendar in pieces all over the kitchen floor. It was a rough week because I ended up having to wing it and just remember the plan. One of the first things I did was order a new calendar. I am super embarrassed to write this—I have actually deleted it several times—but about a month later, Penny ate my new calendar too. It took two calendars for me to learn my lesson. No more calendars on the counter! (And dog-training classes for Penny!)

Trust me. Despite the risk of a dog eating it (or, more likely, someone in your family, including you, spilling coffee or juice on it), using a calendar to set yourself up for success each and every day will make things happen in your classroom and create more time than you have ever had before. In a month's time, I promise—you will be in love with your calendar, *not* your to-do list.

Best of all, I'm gonna make that happen in six easy steps.

Let me show you how!

Step 1 • BUY A HARD-COPY CALENDAR THAT HAS PLENTY OF ROOM FOR DAILY TASKS.

I love pretty calendars! Always have. I used to be obsessed with planners and calendars and organizers. I had *opinions*. Because, to be fair? It's hard not to get caught up in the teacher calendar/planner craze that happens *every* summer. My teacher

Facebook groups are packed full of teachers asking which planner is the best and posting pictures of their planners. Some teachers buy the done-for-you version, while others are printing and hole-punching to create their own perfect-for-them planners.

I am no different from any of these teachers. I *still* love a beautiful calendar! When I was young, I bought a new kitten-themed wall calendar every January and hung it on my bedroom wall. When back-to-school shopping, I would spend way too much time examining every Five Star calendar at Walmart before making my choice.

When I became a teacher, I desperately wanted a fancy planner with a beautiful cover printed with my name. I saw them all over teacher Instagram accounts. The problem? These planners just didn't fit into my teacher budget. I was stuck using the free one that the local teaching store handed out to anyone who made a fifty-dollar purchase. Can you imagine my excitement when one Christmas I found the most gorgeous planner wrapped under the tree? I immediately did what all planner lovers do: I sniffed the pages. If you are a planner lover, then you know what I am talking about. The next day, I loaded up all the kids for a trip to Target in order to get my necessary supplies: flair pens and washi tape. You have to have the perfect supplies for your planner!

The planner was beautiful and I carried it almost everywhere I went. However, I soon learned that this calendar was not a good fit for me. The pages were not customized for me and so I would spend hours every week using the washi tape to make the pages work for my class schedule. The pages looked like layouts from a scrapbook. They were cute, but a teacher does not have time for crafting in her planner every week!

The other problem with my fancy planner was that it only had space for me to plan my school hours. There were boxes for my math, reading, and science lessons, but there wasn't any space to plan my time before school, after school, and during my prep period. When I first drooled over these planners, it never even occurred to me that I needed this kind of space. I was totally focused on planning how every last instructional minute would be spent. I was winging the rest.

I still order a beautiful planner every year. (And I still sniff the pages as soon as it is delivered.) However, I don't just look at the cover. I always choose a planner that has space to plan my entire day. The calendars with hourly slots are the best for increasing your productivity. Lots of companies offer very pretty versions of these calendars! And when you use your flair pens in it, the calendar becomes ten times cuter.

Step 2 • SET ASIDE AN HOUR EVERY WEEKEND TO PLAN YOUR WEEK.

My planning time is on Sunday afternoon. I love planning at this time because it helps me feel like I am starting the new week on the right foot. Other people I know like to plan on Friday afternoon or Sunday evening. You do you. Please note that this is different from lesson planning. We will talk about that later. During this hour, you are going to be planning how you will be using nonteaching time.

When I sit down to plan, I know I am prioritizing myself and my family by making a plan to be productive. To prepare, I grab my calendar and a couple flair pens and do my planning from the couch.

I won't lie, sometimes I feel lazy.

On many Sunday afternoons, I am cuddled up with my soft blanket watching a football game and scrolling through social media. Getting up and grabbing the calendar seems like a lot of work.

Doing the actual planning is challenging on lazy days like these.

There have been times I have just skipped it. I tell myself, "I'll do it first thing Monday morning." But that Monday comes and goes and my calendar pages remain blank. Weeks like that end up being hard. I feel like I am running in two directions and tripping over my own feet. I forget about important tasks and I come home late most days.

After a week like that, I recommit to my weekly planning time. The chaotic week reminds me of how much I need a plan. If I take an hour to plan once per week, I will actually get back hours of free time for myself, my family, and whatever else I want to do. It's worth the effort.

Step 3 • WHEN YOU PLAN YOUR WEEK, DO A BRAIN DUMP.

Sitting on the couch (or at a real desk!) on Friday or Sunday, ask yourself: What do I need to accomplish? Include both personal and teaching related tasks.

But here's the catch: you are not going to do all these things. This particular list is a brain dump, *not* a to-do list. The reason I'm asking you to create this list is to literally empty your brain. I don't know about you, but all day long my brain comes up with tasks that I should do or need to do or want to do. Doing a dump allows your brain to stop storing this information but still keep a record of it. That's what will allow you to relax: you won't constantly be in fear of forgetting something.

Personally, I am epileptic and have been for my entire life. People who are epileptic have unexplained seizures. Every time I have a seizure, I struggle with my memory. I am always worried that I will forget something important. (For what it's worth, the day I wrote this, I forgot that my kids only had a half day of school.) The weekly brain-dump exercise is rewarding for me because I get to release my brain from the responsibility of remembering *everything*.

Here's another hint. As you do the brain dump, do not worry about whether or not the task is a good one or whether you have time. Don't try to make a plan or worry about the length of the list. Just write down every darn thing that comes to your mind. Grade math tests, talk to Allison about field day, email Derrik's mom, make a dentist appointment, et cetera. This dump becomes a bank of things you will choose from when creating your schedule for the week.

Step 4 • CIRCLE THE TASKS THAT ABSOLUTELY MUST BE DONE *THIS* WEEK.

This includes scheduled meetings and appointments and other tasks that have a deadline.

I used to be really, really bad at this—especially when I started teaching. I was hired for my first teaching job just one week before school started. I was overjoyed and immediately packed up the hubby and all four kids for a field trip to my new classroom. We spent the next week decorating that classroom. I chose a circus theme and proceeded to hang bulletin boards with clowns, jugglers, and elephants. (How did I not know that clowns are kind of scary?!)

At the end of the week, my classroom walls were filled. But I had not spent *any* time on the actual teaching part. I hadn't reviewed the reading standards, studied the curriculum, or prepared activities for the first week of school. On my list for that week, decorating was a *must*-do item for me. My brain told me that it was the most important task and that it needed to be done.

My brain lied. If my students had shown up on the first day and the walls had been completely bare, they would not have minded. These were third graders, after all. I just needed to have meaningful activities prepared, some kind of classroom routine, and a collection of engaging picture books to read.

So: don't do what I did. Instead, recognize that when you are looking at your brain dump and trying to decide what the must-do items are, your brain may try to steer you in the wrong direction. There are probably lots of things that would be nice to get finished this week. And there may be things that you find enjoyable and want to do this week. You might have time for some of those tasks.

But for now, circle only items that *must* be completed soon or there will be negative consequences. If report cards are due on Friday, then that goes on the list for the week, preferably before Thursday. If you have an IEP meeting on Thursday, preparing for that is a must-do item. Changing out your bulletin board because you are tired of looking at the elf display in February is *not* a must-do. It would be nice, but if you have to wait another week, you can.

(Mental note: no elf bulletin boards next year!)

Step 5 • SCHEDULE TIME TO COMPLETE THE MOST IMPORTANT TASKS ON YOUR CALENDAR.

Start with the most important tasks and schedule a time to *complete* them on your calendar. This is the sour cream of this chapter. Let me explain. I love Mexican food. I am proud to admit that I eat Mexican food about three or four times per week. No matter what meal I am enjoying—a taco, chimichanga, or enchilada—I *always* put sour cream on top. For me, it is the secret sauce that makes Mexican food go from yummy to ridiculously delicious.

This step in the planning process is the sour cream to increase your productivity. It's the ultimate secret sauce and game changer. Brain dumping and prioritizing are great on their own, but add in some time blocking on your calendar and you have an unbeatable recipe for a week of project completion.

I want you to compare this to your lesson planning. When you plan your instructional minutes for the week, you don't just make a list of standards or lessons that you need to cover. No way! In fact, if you planned like that, you would probably get to Friday every week and realize you were way behind and never going to finish the list.

Instead, you map out each hour of the school day, right? (Right?!) You decide exactly what lesson you will teach, how you will teach it, and what activities your students will complete. If I were to ask you, "What will your students be doing at 9:17 a.m. on Thursday?" you would be able to give me specific details including the workbook page number they would be completing. Most teachers I know block all their instructional time.

But for some reason, it doesn't occur to us to do the same for our plan and prep time! Instead of planning exactly what we will be doing every morning before school, during our prep period, and after school, we are just making long lists of things we hope to accomplish. When Friday comes along, we realize we are way behind and never going to finish the list.

The solution is simple! Let's start planning our prep time.

There are two important keys to this process.

First, break down your tasks into small pieces. Doing so will make them easier for you to fit on your crowded calendar (because we know you don't have much prep time!). We don't want to be scheduling time to *work* on something. Instead we are scheduling time to *complete* something.

You might not have one time block long enough to "work on grades." Instead, break that particular task into mini projects, such as "grade ten math tests" or "enter spelling test scores into the gradebook." The reason this approach works super-duper well is that you are telling your brain exactly what it must complete during a specific time frame.

Instead of saying, "I need to grade my writing samples today," you are declaring exactly when you will do that grading and how long the grading will take. This might feel challenging at first because you aren't used to deciding how long something will take for you to finish. (But remember—you do this all the time with your students!) The thing is, your brain will fill whatever amount of time you give it. So if you tell your mind that it takes all day to get the grading done, it will take all day. If you give yourself an hour and a half, that is precisely how long it will take. The same is true of your students. If you tell them that they have to finish an assignment sometime this week, most will turn it in at 2:59 on Friday afternoon. If you give them one hour to complete the exact same assignment, they will get the same assignment done in significantly less time.

The second key to this process is to schedule each small task to a specific time on your calendar. This will be the time at which you complete the task. You are committing to the plan. You are making a meeting with yourself. Instead of having a list of things to do, you have a time scheduled to complete all your most pressing tasks. And these small tasks are *so* much more likely to get finished!

Here is an example of what that schedule might look like during a week.

Example:

7:45–8:00	*Answer emails*
8:00–9:00	*Teach*
9:00–9:45	*Grade nine writing samples (plan period)*
9:45–2:45	*Teach*

2:45–3:30 *Grade nine writing samples*

3:30–4:00 *Enter writing and reading grades in the gradebook*

4:00–4:15 *Set out materials for tomorrow*

4:15 *Go home*

The more specific you get on your calendar, the more productive you will be with your time!

Step 6 • DROP THE GUILT.

It's not very likely that you will be able to do everything on your brain-dump list.

Most of the time that's just not possible—and that's okay. It's not like you are currently finishing everything on your to-do list. The difference here is that you are being strategic about prioritizing and scheduling the tasks you are completing rather than winging it. You are going to complete so many *important* tasks and that will help you feel accomplished.

Perhaps you already noticed what happened at 4:15 p.m. on the teacher's schedule in the last step. Maybe you laughed at the idea of leaving school that early. But here's the truth. There is no award for being the last car in the parking lot or for working twelve-plus-hour days.

So what do you do with all the items from your brain dump that do not fit on your calendar? You have three options, and I refer to them as the Triple D.

Delay

Some items can be pushed back until next week or even next month. These are items that might be nice to complete, but they are not a top priority based on your definition of teacher success. Your brain might try to convince you that they are important, but the reality is that nothing detrimental will happen if you push these activities into a different week.

Delegate

Are there any tasks on your brain-dump list that you can delegate to someone else? Don't say no too quickly! Too often we think no one can or would want to help us. The reality is that there are many people who care about us and would be willing to do a simple task to show their appreciation. Does your school allow parent volunteers? If so, don't hesitate to ask parents if they would be willing to volunteer to cut lamination, copy papers for next week, grade spelling tests, or organize a cabinet. Do you have older children, nieces, nephews, or neighbors? For a small fee, teenagers can prepare center games, check off papers, sharpen pencils, and prepare supplies for an upcoming art project.

Tasks Volunteers Can Help With in the Classroom

- Grading simple assignments that include an answer key

- Photocopying

- Printing materials

- Laminating or cutting lamination

- Stapling or hole-punching

- Organizing a shelf or a cabinet

- Preparing materials for a craft or a project

- Taking down or putting up a new bulletin board display

- Planning and preparing for classroom parties and celebrations

- Checking off who has completed homework or classwork

- Reading with a student or a small group

- Helping a small group with a center activity

- Playing a game with a small group

- Helping a student who was absent

- Administering sight-word assessments

- Downloading apps onto devices

Delete

When we are brain dumping, we write down every single thing that comes to our mind. Now that we are prioritizing and scheduling, it's easier to see items we really don't need to do. An item in this category may have been something your neighbor teacher did that you liked or something you saw on social media. It might have seemed like a good idea, but now that you are looking at your calendar, you realize it just doesn't fit. And that is perfectly okay! Cross it off the list and move on.

Go through the rest of your brain dump and decide what will be delayed, delegated, and deleted. Instead of feeling guilty about the things you won't be doing this week, choose to celebrate your ability to prioritize, schedule, and let go!

When I mention this system to teachers, there are usually a few questions. But luckily, I always come prepared—with answers.

Q: What if you have no idea how long a task will take to complete?

A: I get that. At first, you might not know how long each of your tasks will take. If you are used to grading while watching Netflix, you might know exactly how long (one episode) and you might not. Multitasking, whether you're relaxing and watching a TV show or helping the kids out with their homework, can make it seem like you spent the entire night grading.

My suggestion is to start out by deciding how long you *want* to spend on a certain task. Schedule that amount of time and do your very best to complete the task in the given time. At the end of the week, reflect on what worked and what did not work. If you could not finish a task in the allotted time, you can choose either to get

> "My husband used to grade my math papers. The kids knew if there was a mistake in my grading, it was his fault. He has cut, laminated, and hauled many things. It takes a special man to be a teacher's husband!"
>
> —Raegan B.

"After many years of unhealthy habits, I decided to change how I did things! I'll stay late in the very beginning of the year while doing the initial classroom setup, but after that, I'm only allowed to stay after dark one day a week and I never go in on the weekends." —Camille P.

faster and more focused the next time or to give yourself longer the next time. Easy peasy.

Q: What if stuff pops up during the week that I didn't plan for?

A: If? I can guarantee you that things you didn't plan for will pop up at school. It's a matter of when, not if. A parent will demand a meeting, a student will need a packet of work for the two weeks he will be absent, and your partner teacher will have an unexpected absence and ask you to help her substitute. Sounds like a typical week for a teacher.

The best thing you can do is expect the unexpected. Add some flex time to your calendar each week. Block out a couple of thirty-minute time slots for the tasks and meetings that pop up and wreak havoc on your calendar. Now you can use that flex time for the unexpected task or you can move tasks to that flex time if you have to attend a meeting when you planned to grade or lesson plan.

I like to schedule flex time on Friday afternoons. If I don't have a lot of fires to put out and I keep focused and finish the items on my calendar, then I can reward myself by going home a little earlier! This turns into something I am willing to work extra hard for during the week. Getting my Friday afternoon free becomes a little competition with myself.

Implementing this system is an easy, practical way to help you make the most of your time while also identifying areas where you're absolutely wasting time or doing things (like creating endless to-do lists) that are self-defeating. If you want to stop the madness, start here. I promise this will transform your life and allow you to go home before dark.

Time-Waster to Time-Saver

As teachers, we are always looking for time-saving strategies! Finding ways to get your must-do tasks completed faster can give you the opportunity to go home earlier.

One task that can take up a lot of time is your email and parent communication. A great time-saver is creating templates for any type of communication you will do multiple times during the year. Write a basic version of each email now and keep it in your drafts so that you can pull it up, copy and paste, make little changes, and use it over and over again throughout the year.

Here are some templates you might consider creating:

- Parent-teacher-conference announcements, reminders, and sign-ups
- Asking for supplies
- Class party needs
- Missing assignments
- Half-day or no-school reminder
- Reminder that an at-home project is due soon

There are probably several other email templates you can create that are specific to your classroom needs. Having these emails ready and waiting will help you save a little time here and a little time there. It all adds up!

If you have time to do only one thing
from this chapter, I want you to:

Schedule tasks by how long they take to complete.

So often we think to ourselves, "Today I need to work on my grading." The problem is that we are not deciding exactly when we will grade and how much grading we are going to complete during that time. Even if we do get some grading completed, we won't know if we were truly successful. Deciding exactly what we will complete during a time block makes it easier to see and celebrate our productivity.

The Not So Wimpy Way to Ditch Your To-Do List

1. Buy a hard-copy calendar with lots of room for daily tasks (pages 40–42).

2. Set aside an hour every weekend to plan the next week (pages 42–43).

3. Do a weekly brain dump and classify tasks as:

   Important (only *you* can do)

   Delay (you can do this later)

   Delegate (someone else can do it)

   Delete (pages 49–51)

4. Schedule time to complete the most important tasks (pages 45–47).

5. Stick to your calendar!

CHAPTER THREE

· · · · · · · · · · · · · · · · · ·

Batch Your Lesson Plans

uring my first year teaching, I won a cruise.

When I found out, I was in a staff meeting. I was jumping up and down and acting like a fool. I called my husband in front of the entire staff. A cruise seemed so unreal to us. At the time we had four kids, we both worked multiple jobs, and we had lots of debt. We didn't have the luxury of traveling. The cruise was such a treat. We dreamed about dinners in a fancy dining room, time by the ocean with adult beverages, and evenings dancing.

At least, that is what I *thought* we would be doing.

In truth, I spent time every afternoon of that dream cruise lesson planning.

Yup, I was planning out my test prep lessons because standardized testing was just a couple weeks away. I used bar napkins to write down my lesson ideas. (Can you believe I forgot my lesson-plan book and flair pens?) I was lesson planning instead of taking a break and enjoying some much-needed time with my husband. In fact, I was actually boring him to death by talking about the science unit I wanted to start after break. Thank goodness he is a great sport and did not push me overboard.

Maybe you have never lesson planned on a cruise, but I am certain that you can think of dozens of times you were lesson planning when you know you should have been spending that time with family or taking care of yourself. Have you lesson planned over holiday breaks? Have you lesson planned on someone's birthday? Have you lesson planned at your kids' soccer games? You're not alone. I bet everyone reading this book is currently nodding their head. As teachers, we have all too often prioritized lesson planning over living our lives.

If you've ended up lesson planning on a Sunday night, this chapter is for you! You're not alone if you are so tired and busy during the week that you end up having to create math lessons for the week at 4:00 p.m. on a Sunday—not to mention reading and social studies and science too. The worst part about planning right before you need to teach is that you end up looking for fun ways to teach whatever it is on Pinterest or Googling to find a good activity. Next thing you know you're on Amazon pricing Hula-Hoops you'll use only once.

That, my friend, is a loooonnnnggggg way to create lesson plans, because you're coming up with new activities every week, which takes several hours every week.

It's time to spend less time lesson planning!

I would love to say that I had an epiphany moment while lesson planning on my cruise.

But I didn't. It took me years to realize that the key to spending less time lesson planning is *batching*. Let me explain this by referring to something I really like: cookies. You are sitting at home watching your favorite show on Netflix and you have a sweet tooth. You head to the kitchen to make your very favorite chocolate chip cookies.

Do you just make a couple for tonight?

And then maybe you can make a couple more tomorrow night?

No!

That would be crazy time-consuming. Making cookies twice would mean you'd have to do everything twice. Get out all the ingredients twice. Do the mixing and the baking twice. Not to mention you would have to clean up all the dishes twice.

That's why we bake in batches. When we make a whole lot of cookies at once, you only need to prepare once. You only have to wait for them to bake once. And you only have to wash the dishes once. And with even a sliver of willpower, you can still have cookies both nights.

The same approach can work for lesson planning. Instead of sitting down week after week to plan out the next week's reading, writing, math, science, and social studies, I'll show you how to batch that work to create *five weeks of a single subject* at once.

WHY BATCHING IS THE BEST

There are so many great reasons to adopt the habit of batching.

I have never met a teacher who complained that they had too much time and not enough to do. Saving time is a huge benefit of batching your lesson plans.

This is what lesson planning looks like when using the traditional method: you grab your reading textbook, a pacing guide (if you have one), read alouds, and a few center activities. You try to plan for Monday, but the first ten minutes are spent staring at a blank screen, then typing something and immediately deleting it. About ten minutes in, you start to find your groove, and the remaining days of reading plans go a lot faster.

Then you have to stop and grab your math textbook, pacing guide, and some worksheets, and open a few websites you like to use. Or maybe you spend an hour scrolling through Pinterest. Once again, you are stuck when it comes to the first day or two of lessons. It takes a while to find your groove again.

Task switching is time-consuming! Just getting out different materials for each subject takes up time. But even *more* time is consumed getting your brain in the flow. When you switch from one subject to another, it takes your brain some time to catch up. Lessons that should be relatively easy to plan end up taking twice as long.

When you batch, you are focusing only on one subject. You only need to get out one set of materials. It will still be challenging to get started, but once you get going, your brain will be able to stay focused on the one task and stay in a flow. According to *Psychology Today*,* we take only about a tenth of a second to switch tasks, but that switch can reduce our productivity by 40 percent! Basically, when we switch tasks, we use different parts of our brain, which tires us out way quicker than when we're focused on a single task at a time. And that doesn't even include having to pull out different materials every few minutes.

A fantastic reason to adopt the habit of batching your lesson plans is that it leads to higher-quality plans. The majority of your lesson plans will be created from that state of flow. This is when your brain will do the best work, because it is more focused. The lesson plans you write last-minute on Sunday night while watching your latest Netflix obsession are almost never your best work.

Another bonus of batching your lesson plans is that you will have more time to

---

*Susan Weinschenk, "The True Cost of Multi-Tasking," *Psychology Today*, September 18, 2012, https://www.psychologytoday.com/us/blog/brain-wise/201209/the-true-cost-multi-tasking.

prep for the actual lesson. If you need materials from the store, you will have time to grab them the next time you grocery shop. This means you won't have to make a last-minute trip after school when you are exhausted and wearing a Ms. Frizzle dress that was the perfect addition to your science lesson that day.

If you need to make copies, you will have time to plan a photocopy session. This means you won't be waiting in a long line on Monday morning stressing because the person in front of you is making copies of every single spelling list for the entire year. The extra prep time will also allow you to laminate materials so that you can use them year after year.

Getting ahead on your lesson plans means materials can be prepped during school time rather than during personal time. Not to mention starting your week without materials and feeling unprepared is super stressful!

START WITH PACING

Before we jump into planning lessons, we need to talk about how to break down an entire school year into semesters, quarters, weeks, and individual days.

In my early days teaching, I was winging it. I would think, "At this pace, are we going to cover all of the standards before testing? I sure hope so! We will find out soon enough."

This usually resulted in tons of stress at the end of the year when I discovered we needed to squeeze two whole math units into the last week. Sound familiar?

It's sort of crazy how little help we get about how we should teach students everything in a school year. One time, my school gave us teachers a list of what we had to teach our students that calendar year . . . but that was it. Another time, an administrator in my district said that she should be able to walk into any third-grade classroom and that all the teachers should be doing the exact same lesson at the exact same time. But she didn't give us a schedule, so I'm still not sure how that was supposed to work.

The best preparation I received was when my district gathered a couple teachers from each grade level and had us create a full-year pacing guide for reading, writing, and math. My mind was blown! This document was like getting a copy of my own treasure map. I actually had a map that helped me pace out my lessons for the year. If the map said I had three weeks to work on fractions, then I knew I was on track if I spent a full three weeks on that unit. No more guessing and scrambling.

But most schools don't work that way.

Thanks to Common Core, most states in the United States have similar standards when it comes to what skills students need to learn at each grade level. Using those standards, teachers figure out how much time to spend on a particular skill—for instance, teaching multiplication in third grade, as I did.

Having a map will make lesson planning faster because you no longer have to make decisions about timing. Should I spend one week on nouns or two? Should we start with fiction standards or nonfiction standards? All of these decisions are made already! You are actually batching all the pacing decisions.

If you already have a pacing guide, you are among the lucky ones. Go do a little happy dance. If you do not have a pacing guide, you aren't alone. (You can still do a happy dance if you want.) Most districts do not provide this resource for all subject areas. The good news is that you can create your own pacing guide. It's not hard! Making the decisions in one sitting is so much easier than having to come back to pacing every single week when you are doing your planning.

Start with one subject at a time.

1. *Break the subject into units of study. For example, for math you might have to teach your students topics like place value, addition, subtraction, multiplication, fractions, et cetera.*

2. *Break these units down into more specific lessons. In your multiplication unit you will have lessons on repeated addition, equal groups, arrays, and so on.*

3. *Write the number of weeks you would like to spend on each unit. Pretend it is your dream world and you have all the time that you want.*

4. *Calculate the number of weeks you actually have for teaching this subject. Remember to take into account things like the first week of school, Thanksgiving, spring break, and testing.*

5. *Determine the difference between the actual number of weeks you have to teach and your dream number of weeks. Start carefully editing the number of weeks based on your reality. Play with these numbers until you feel comfortable. Or at least as comfortable as possible, because we all know that there is never enough time!*

6. *Put dates next to each unit and/or lesson.*

Now you have your very own pacing guide! Will it be perfect?

Nope. In fact, I can guarantee you will find problems with the pacing during the year. Just make notes and adjust the pacing guide each year. It's an evolving document that serves as a map rather than a written-in-stone document you must vow to live by.

If you are struggling to create your own pacing guide, check out notsowimpyteacher.com /bookresources for a free pacing guide that's appropriate for your grade level.

Once you have your pacing guide, take out a calendar. Map out how many weeks you expect to spend on each unit. (And yes—I know timing changes based on the unique needs of your learners. We are simply outlining a plan that's meant to be flexible. I'll talk about how to adjust these plans later on.)

Now you are ready to batch!

HOW TO BATCH LESSON PLANS

A typical lesson planning session includes creating plans for one week for five different subjects. Batching your lesson plans is different from the traditional lesson planning because you are creating several weeks of plans for just one subject. There are two different ways to batch your lesson plans, and you will want to choose the recipe that best fits your personality. I recommend trying both before you decide what you'll use moving forward.

Let's go back to the cookies I mentioned earlier. I believe there are two different types of chocolate chip cookie bakers. Which one are you? I am the kind of person that buys premade cookie dough. This works for me because I don't have to think much about how to make the cookies and the results are exactly the same every time. This is how the five-week batching plan works. Every batching week looks the same and produces the same results. You are always creating five weeks of lesson plans during your lesson planning time. You don't have to think much about the plan because it doesn't change week to week. It's as simple as done-for-you cookie dough.

Some people make the cookies from scratch using the Toll House recipe. You have to admit that these cookies are more work, but they are so freakin' delicious. This baker has to do a little more planning to get ingredients, measuring, mixing, and dishes. The extra effort is worth it for this person. This is how the unit batching plan works. With this plan, you will create a batch of lesson plans for an entire unit within one subject. It's the ultimate time-saver because you aren't batching only for a specific subject; all the lessons you are planning are related in some way. This means your brain can focus on just one topic. And when you finish the batching session, you won't have to plan for that unit ever again. All your opinion-writing lessons could be completed in one planning session! All your fraction lessons could be completed in another planning session.

The unit batching method takes a little more planning effort because every unit isn't the same length. One week, you might plan a three-week unit for reading, and another week, you might plan a five-week unit for math. You will have to keep track of this on your calendar so that you don't unexpectedly run out of math lesson plans and have to do last-minute planning on Sunday night. That said, the unit batching plan makes it very easy to save the plans from a unit and reuse them for next year! Just imagine how fast lesson planning will be next year when all you need to do is pull up your multiplication plan file and make minor adjustments.

Which type of batching should you do? That really depends on your preference and your personality. If you prefer a simple, predictable routine that requires the same amount of effort, time, and lessons produced each week, then you will probably like the five-week batching plan. But be aware that this method might have you lesson planning multiple topics in one planning session. For instance, you could plan addition, subtraction, and multiplication lessons during the same day. If that doesn't bother you, this might be the plan for you.

Some people like to organize their thoughts and lessons thematically. Their vision is more big picture and they prefer to tackle all the lessons in one unit at a time. If it's going to drive you crazy to stop lesson planning in the middle of a unit, or after week three of a four-week unit, you might prefer the unit batching plan.

With this plan, you'll know that at the end of your batching session you will have completed every lesson you needed for the whole unit, whether that's geometry or plants. But you'll have to be more flexible with your batching sessions because not all units are exactly the same length. You'll also have to be very organized and keep detailed notes about when you need to plan the next unit. If this doesn't sound like you, you might want to stick with the five-week batching plan.

The reality is that both batching plans are time-savers. I just want you to be honest with yourself and choose the strategy that you are most likely to be successful with and continue using all year. If you're still not sure which will work best for you, pick the one that resonates with you the most. If you love it, great! If not, try the other method. Even if you switch batching methods, you'll still be ahead of the game.

Now that you've chosen your batching style, here are the recipes.

Five-Week Batching Recipe

WEEK 1:

Create five weeks of lesson plans for math.

WEEK 2:

Create five weeks of lesson plans for reading.

WEEK 3:

Create five weeks of lesson plans for writing and grammar.

WEEK 4:

Create five weeks of lesson plans for science.

WEEK 5:

Create five weeks of lesson plans for social studies.

This is the basic recipe, but as with most recipes, you can make small modifications to make it just right for you. You can easily switch the order of planning around if it would make it easier. Would you like to have a week with zero lesson planning? Or do you need to plan for an additional subject? No problem! During week four, you can do five weeks of lesson plans for science and social studies. Now week five can become a lesson plan free week or the week that you use to plan that extra subject.

Unit Batching Recipe

I'll give you a basic idea of how this strategy works, but remember that every unit is a different length. You are going to have to constantly map out the length of the units you have planned and make the needed decision about what subject must be planned each week.

WEEK 1:

Create the lesson plans for your multiplication unit (four weeks).

WEEK 2:

Create the lesson plans for your character traits unit (two weeks).
Create the lesson plans for your point-of-view unit (two weeks).

WEEK 3:

Create the lesson plans for your personal narrative unit (eight weeks).

WEEK 4:

Create the lesson plans for your geography unit (four weeks).

WEEK 5:

Create the lesson plans for your division unit (four weeks).

With this batching plan, I would recommend using a color-coded system to mark in your calendar the weeks that you have planned for each subject. It's more work tracking, but you'll reap the benefits too. You are allowing your brain to get in a deep flow, saving time, and creating unit lesson plans that can be used year after year.

SCHEDULING YOUR BATCHING

I generally bake cookies when I get a craving for a cookie. I rarely plan it out. (Part of adulting is keeping sugar and chocolate chips in the pantry at all times.) Cookies for dinner is not a premeditated meal-planning kind of decision.

I guess that is where the cookie baking and lesson planning analogy has to end. You cannot just decide to whip up a batch of lesson plans when you are in the mood. That is just way too risky and is bound to lead to some late Sunday nights doing the last-minute, bare-minimum planning. To be successful with lesson plan batching and save yourself hours and hours of time this year, you will need to schedule the time on your calendar to do the planning.

I highly recommend that you do all five weeks' worth of plans in one sitting. This will take less time overall because you will be allowing your brain to get into a flow and you will need to get materials out only once. You will want to look at your week and find a day when you can spend one to two hours doing uninterrupted lesson planning. (Lesson planning at your son's tae kwon do practice is not going to cut it.) Choose a day and time and commit to protecting that time.

HOW TO GET STARTED WITH BATCHING

I'm not going to sugarcoat it: getting batching started is going to be tough. It will actually take more time up front to get your lesson plans completed. The challenge is that you need lesson plans for every subject for next week and you need to spend time batching five weeks of one subject or batching a unit for one subject. It's double duty. But that is a short-term challenge, and it will be well worth the long-term benefits we already discussed. I wanted to be open and honest about the struggles of getting started because I don't want you to give up before you've even seen the fruit of your labor. Let's make a deal. I'll give you a plan for getting the batching started if you commit to not quit during the first five weeks. Do we have a deal?

The plan below is for the first five weeks, when you need to plan for your immediate lessons and you are batching for the future lessons. You will need two lesson planning sessions per week during this transitional time. You will start to notice that each week gets a tad easier than the last!

WEEK 1:

PLANNING DAY ONE: *Create one week of lesson plans for reading, writing, science, and social studies.*

PLANNING DAY TWO: *Create five weeks of lesson plans for math.*

WEEK 2:

PLANNING DAY ONE: *Create one week of lesson plans for writing, science, and social studies.*

PLANNING DAY TWO: *Create five weeks of lesson plans for reading.*

WEEK 3:

PLANNING DAY ONE: *Create one week of lesson plans for science and social studies.*

PLANNING DAY TWO: *Create five weeks of lesson plans for writing.*

WEEK 4:

PLANNING DAY ONE: *Create one week of lesson plans for social studies.*

PLANNING DAY TWO: *Create five weeks of lesson plans for science.*

WEEK 5:

PLANNING DAY ONE: *Create five weeks of lesson plans for social studies.*

The following week, you will start with the official batching plan by creating another five weeks of math lesson plans. You are officially batching now!

If you are using the unit batching plan, you will use a similar plan. On the second lesson planning day for each week, you will plan out an entire unit for one subject. It might look something like:

WEEK 1:

> PLANNING DAY ONE: *Create one week of lesson plans for reading, writing, science, and social studies.*

> PLANNING DAY TWO: *Create a four-week unit of math lesson plans.*

WEEK 2:

> PLANNING DAY ONE: *Create one week of lesson plans for writing, science, and social studies.*

> PLANNING DAY TWO: *Create a two-week unit of reading lesson plans.*

WEEK 3:

> PLANNING DAY ONE: *Create one week of lesson plans for science and social studies.*

> PLANNING DAY TWO: *Create an eight-week unit of lesson plans for writing.*

WEEK 4:

> PLANNING DAY ONE: *Create one week of lesson plans for science and social studies.*

> PLANNING DAY TWO: *Create a two-week unit of lesson plans for reading.*

WEEK 5:

> PLANNING DAY ONE: *Create a four-week unit of lesson plans for science and social studies.*

You will notice that this plan is not as routine. I threw in a second unit of reading lesson plans to illustrate the fact that units will vary in length and so you will need to carefully map out the weeks that you have planned.

ADJUSTING FOR STUDENT NEEDS

Anytime I do training about batching for a group of teachers, there is at least one person who will say something like, "I don't batch my lesson plans because I want my lesson plans to be based on student needs, and I don't know what they will need four weeks from now." That is a very relevant point! It's just one of the many reasons I deeply love teachers. You always want your lessons to be personalized and differentiated for your specific learners. It makes sense that you might be nervous to plan your entire multiplication unit when you are not sure how those first few lessons will go.

I would never suggest that lesson plans be written in stone. I would never recommend that you don't adjust for student needs. But do you want to know the truth? It's so much easier to make these adjustments when you have an entire unit of plans in front of you! You can easily add an extra lesson if you notice that the majority of your students are still struggling with a skill. It will take far less time to write that one lesson than to write an entire week of lessons. You can just push back the lessons you have already created.

A good rule of thumb is to include thirty minutes each week on your calendar for reviewing the lessons you are teaching the following week. This time is great for refamiliarizing yourself with lessons you may have written weeks ago. It is also great for noticing places where you'd like to modify a lesson or add an extra lesson.

MORE TIME-SAVING TIPS FOR LESSON PLANNING

Make routines your friend.

In those early years of teaching, I still believed the myth that the greatest teachers were doing all the things in the classroom. I desperately wanted to prove to myself that I could be an amazing teacher, and so I spent a significant amount of my lesson planning time sifting through Pinterest. I would spend hours creating boards and pinning every gorgeous and unique lesson that I could find. (And let's be honest, I would also get distracted and start pinning recipes I would never make and DIY home projects I would never have the time or patience to tackle.)

After doing all the pinning, I would start asking myself questions like: What's something fun I can do this week in math? What would be a unique way to practice grammar this week? Are there any cute writing projects my students can make this week?

I worked so hard to make sure that every week was different from the last. If no two weeks were the same, I would surely deserve one of those World's Best Teacher coffee mugs. (I may not drink coffee, but I still want to deserve the mug!)

As you can imagine, lesson planning for each week was very time-consuming. I was spending an entire day researching and preparing all new activities.

Humor me for a moment. Have you ever shown up to your usual grocery store only to find that they completely rearranged the entire store? Isn't it frustrating? You can't find a darn thing. The shopping trip takes twice as long as usual and you end up leaving without your favorite granola bars because you could not find them and you couldn't bring yourself to ask for help *again.* Your entire shopping routine was thrown out the window. Can you just imagine if the store management decided to rearrange every single week?

That is exactly what I was doing to myself and my students when I was lesson planning. I was changing everything every week. My students never knew what to expect. This led to lower-quality work and significantly less independence and confidence from my students. Plus, all of the changes were extremely time-consuming for me. I felt like the grocery store worker who had to switch the cereal aisle with the baking aisle.

The solution is simple. To save loads of time planning your lessons, make routines your friend. Instead of adding something new to your lessons every week, your goal should be to make each week look almost identical to the week before. If I walked into your classroom at the same time every Tuesday, I would see nearly the exact same activity happening in your classroom.

For some subjects, you might choose to have weekly routines. This means that every day may not be the same but every Monday is the same as the next Monday. Tuesday might be a little different than Monday, but every Tuesday is the same. I used weekly routines for grammar and vocabulary.

GRAMMAR:

MONDAY: *Introduce a new skill with a PowerPoint lesson*

TUESDAY: *Interactive notebook activity*

WEDNESDAY: *Short writing prompts*

THURSDAY: *Whole-class task-card scoot*

FRIDAY: *Assessment*

VOCABULARY:

MONDAY: *Introduce the words with definitions and sentences*

TUESDAY: *Add antonyms and synonyms for each word*

WEDNESDAY: *Break words into prefix, root, and suffix*

THURSDAY: *Draw pictures to represent each word*

FRIDAY: *Assessment*

For other subjects you might have a daily routine. This means that every day will look almost identical. I had daily routines for writing and math.

WRITING:

MINI LESSON   *10 minutes*

INDEPENDENT WRITING   *25 minutes*

SHARING WRITING   *5 minutes*

MATH:

MATH FACTS   *2 minutes*

WARM-UP   *3 minutes*

MINI LESSON   *15 minutes*

PRACTICE SHEET   *10 minutes*

FIRST SMALL-GROUP/CENTER ROTATION   *30 minutes*

SECOND SMALL-GROUP/CENTER ROTATION   *30 minutes*

Why do weekly and daily routines make lesson planning faster?

First, you will no longer need to spend hours sifting through Pinterest and Instagram to find new activities each week. You will no longer have to read directions and figure out how to prepare and implement all these new activities. My routines include using task cards and interactive notebooks. I researched and learned how to use both these activities. Now the activities can be used for the entire year without additional research. Since I know that I will need task cards and interactive-notebook activities for the entire year, I can look for a bundle that includes materials for the entire year. That means no more last-minute online-shopping sessions. Once I own the bundle, I can start preparing them in bulk so that I am not printing, laminating, and cutting late on Sunday night. When I go to fill in my lesson plan book, I never have to ask myself, "What should I do in grammar this week?" I know what I am doing in grammar every day for the rest of the year!

Writing Substitute Teacher Lesson Plans

"Ugh! I feel like death warmed over. Even though I feel terrible, it would still be worse to plan for a substitute than to just go to school sick."

–Jamie S. (Me! Lol.)

"Before Covid, I sent my kids to school sick because I couldn't take the day off. It wasn't because my admin couldn't find me a sub but because it would take me forever to write the sub plans and go in and prep everything."

–Kjirsten W.

"Once, I got in a car accident on my way to school. First call was 911, second was my principal, third was my husband informing him I was fine. I got hit head-on, my car was totaled—but I had the state police officer drop me off at school. My principal, my husband, and the school nurse forced me to go to the hospital, but not before I had made sub plans and copies! 🫠"

—Jennifer L.

"I was 37 weeks pregnant and had some bleeding in the morning. I didn't have my long-term sub plans finished yet, I knew the kids needed me, so I got ready for the day and headed into work like nothing was happening. Ended up having to go to the hospital because I was in active labor with my daughter, who was born the next day!"

—Cristina L.

If you have ever had a similar thought about creating substitute teacher plans, then it is time to create a better system and templates! If you take the time to prepare when you are healthy, you will never have to deal with the overwhelm of planning when you are sick or have to miss school unexpectedly.

The biggest mistake and time-waster we make when preparing for a substitute is creating a plan that is completely different from the plan we regularly use. We change up the routine and all the activities because we believe that a substitute would never teach it as well as we could. That may be true in some cases, but when we change the routine in our classroom, we make the day significantly more challenging for our students and our substitute. Our students have gotten used to our daily and weekly routines. They know how to be successful with the activities they are used to completing. When they change, suddenly our students need more assistance and are more likely to be off task. This makes for a crazy day for the substitute. Trust me! I was a substitute on and off for twelve years before becoming a full-time teacher.

The best thing you can do for your substitute and your students is to keep the routine and activities the same as a typical day. The great news is that this makes planning for the substitute much easier because you have already planned the day and you don't need to come up with new activities to keep students busy all day.

Now, the bad news is that you can't just hand your lesson plan to a substitute. It's generally not specific enough for a guest teacher. The solution is to create a detailed lesson plan template for each day of the week. Since you have daily and weekly routines now, each Monday will look almost the same. So you can create a Monday template that includes every detail of your typical Monday. Do the same for each of the other days. Save these templates in an easy-to-access location. When you need to take a day off, open the template and add any details that are specific to that particular day, such as page numbers or the read-aloud title. This should take less than ten minutes because you already took time to create a template! You can also check out notsowimpyteacher.com/bookresources for free substitute teacher lesson plan templates.

Use a lesson plan template.

You already know that I have a serious love for cute planners and colorful pens. You probably won't be surprised to learn that I spent hours and hours using stickers and washi tape to make my lesson planner look cute. It was a beautiful masterpiece . . . and a *huge* waste of time!

Using a quality lesson plan template can save you tons of time. The key is to save everything in the template that you repeat regularly. If you need to document page numbers from the teacher manual every day for math, make sure your template includes "Teacher manual page #" for every day of the week. If you will be referencing a lesson number each day for writing, make sure that your template has "Lesson #" saved for every day of writing. If you do a task-card scoot in grammar every Thursday, make sure that is saved to your lesson plan template for every week. Never waste time retyping something each and every week. (For examples, check out notsowimpyteacher.com/bookresources.)

Buy resource bundles.

When I asked the Not So Wimpy Teacher community on Facebook what the biggest lesson plan time sucker is, they overwhelmingly agreed that it was finding good resources. Before I became a teacher, I assumed that teachers were given all of the resources that they needed. I thought that the school would provide textbooks, workbooks, games, and crafts. Yup, I was sadly mistaken. Anyone else?

The reality is that even if our school provides some curriculum, we almost always need to supplement it to make lessons more engaging and to meet the diverse needs of our learners. There is also a very good chance that our school will provide a curriculum for one subject but nothing for another subject. Or maybe you have a curriculum, but it is so old and outdated that Pluto is still listed as a planet. Been there and have the shirt to prove it.

Finding the resources is time-consuming. I would waste hours on Pinterest and Teachers Pay Teachers trying to find that perfect activity that I could actually afford. Until I found the activity, it was virtually impossible to complete my lesson plans for the week. Each week I was starting from zero. I needed new resources for virtually every subject.

One week, I had a weak moment and I bought an entire bundle of reading passages. It cost more than I was used to paying. Most weeks I would search and search until I found a free passage that met the needs of my students. This week, I was not in the mood to dig. I just wanted something quick. The bundle was so good! Not only did I have the passage I needed for this week, I now had passages for the entire school year. I could basically plug in the weekly close-reading activity on my lesson plans for the rest of the year. This was so satisfying!

After this experience, I decided to make a list of all of the materials I like to use in my daily and weekly class routines. I spent some time searching and researching until I found bundles of task cards, math centers, interactive notebooks, and more.

Yes, purchasing bundles of resources was an up-front investment. I definitely did my research, asked questions, and read product feedback. I wanted to make the best decisions. It felt pricey at first, but it ended up saving a huge amount.

First, I saved money in the long run. I loved to look for free resources, but the reality is that free was not always possible or the best fit for my students. So I would end up buying a three-dollar resource here and a five-dollar resource there. This really added up over time! In fact, those small purchases every week or two ended up costing more than my bundles. Even more important, the bundles were a savings in time. When I went to batch, I had a collection of quality resources that were easy to plug into my lesson plans. I spent considerably less time searching for resources each week. My time is valuable. Your time is valuable! Bundles save time. You can shop for our resource bundles at notsowimpyteacher.com/store.

Collaborate with your team.

Which student were you in high school? Your teacher announces that you will be completing a project in small groups and it will be worth a big chunk of your grade. Are you the student who is super excited and starts looking around the room to make eye contact with your best friends? Or are you the student who immediately feels heaviness because you know you will need to do most of the work in order to get the grade you want? I'm a crazy perfectionist, so I was definitely the second student. I pulled the load on most group assignments. I tried to keep everyone on task and encouraged everyone in the group to share their ideas. But in the end, I volunteered to complete almost every part of the project because I knew it was the only way to get the project completed on time.

Collaborating with your team or a teammate to create lesson plans can be an amazing time-saver and it can also be a huge time waster. It will depend on two things: the people you work with and the systems you create.

First, I want to give you permission *not* to collaborate with teammates to batch your lesson plans. It is not always a good fit. If you work with teachers who are amazing, but they have a very different teaching style from yours, the lesson plans they create will probably not work well in your classroom. You can say no thank you. Maybe your teammate is a bit of a procrastinator and they will probably write their portion of the lesson plans late on Sunday night. That will create stress for you. You can say no thank you. Maybe your team is made up of the nicest people, but they are pretty dang chatty. I call these people Chatty McChattersons. These types of teammates are well-meaning, but they often make projects take longer rather than saving time. You can say no thank you.

Saying no does not make you a bad team player. It's quite the opposite. Saying no means that you care too much about your teammates to want to waste their time with a collaboration that is not in everyone's best interest. You're pretty amazing like that.

On the other hand, maybe you work with a teammate who has a very similar teaching style and she also wants to get the lesson planning done quicker and earlier. In this case, collaboration can be a huge time-saver. Having a few systems in place from the beginning will ensure that this is a fantastic collaboration that divides the work without multiplying the stress. The goal is to have quality lesson plans that take half the time to create and still have a coworker friendship at the end of the year.

First, you will want to divide up the work. The best way to do this is to assign certain subjects to each person in the collaboration. Start by discussing what subject everyone considers to be their zone of genius. Some teachers feel totally in their element teaching reading, while others feel like a rock star during math class. You will get the best quality of work from everyone in the collaboration if they are assigned the subject they feel most confident with.

Next, the best way to save time with this collaboration is to agree to do the work independently. I have been in lesson plan collaborations where we would meet every week and work together to write the plans for the following week. The meetings would be so long and typically the plans were not complete at the end of the meeting. When we get together to work, we distract one another. Just as we are getting in the flow, someone interrupts to tell a story about a student licking his classmate's shoe. This turns into a whole gabfest where everyone shares the craziest thing a student has done in their classroom. Thirty minutes later, you get back to the lesson planning. Collaborations like this actually take more time than doing all the planning on your own.

Instead, split up the work and do it separately. This way you can work in a quiet environment of your choosing. This might be at your desk after school or on the couch later that night. The key is that you must decide on a due date and everyone must commit to adhering to the due date each week. Perhaps lesson plans for the next week are due every Wednesday. This gives you time to read them over and ask any questions that you might have.

Finally, agree on what must be included in the lesson plans. Failing to do this before you get started can lead to frustration if you feel like you aren't getting everything you need or that you are doing more work than your partners. Get together and talk about the expectations. Do you have a certain lesson plan template that will be used? Are you responsible for creating assessments? Are you expecting objectives and standards to be included? Do you need a script or bullet points? Is the person required to make copies for their subject area or just write the plans? Hammer all this out in the beginning. I promise that an uncomfortable talk at the start can help you avoid drama all year.

I've shared lots of strategies, and now it is time to put your pen to the paper. Taking action and making decisions now will increase the probability of putting these strategies into action later when you have completed the entire book.

You are not going to be that teacher doing lesson plans during a vacation!

Taking action now will help you to avoid the overwhelm later. I promise!

. . . .

If you have time to do only one thing from this chapter, I want you to:

Choose a batching plan and commit to it by adding it to your calendar.

Everything else in this chapter will add to that and help you optimize, but ultimately what will make the biggest difference for you—by saving time, eliminating stress, and avoiding that line at the copier on Monday morning—is choosing a way to batch your lesson plans and actually doing it for a quarter. Consistently. That's all you have to do.

I'm not gonna lie—that "simple" change might be really challenging. It may take a few weeks or even a couple months to get the hang of batching your lesson plans—and that's okay. But once you start to really get into the flow, you will no longer feel that anxiety on Sunday night about what you're going to teach the next morning, the next week, or even the next month.

You'll know you've got your batching down pat when you don't have to lesson plan on the weekend anymore at all . . . and that you're totally crushing it when you can skip the line at the school copier on a Monday morning.

. . . .

The Not So Wimpy Way to Batch Lesson Plans

1. Create or find a pacing guide for each subject you teach (pages 61–63).

2. Choose a batching plan (pages 64–68).

3. Schedule your batching (pages 68–69).

Optional:

- Create classroom routines (pages 73–76).

- Use a lesson plan template (page 79).

- Buy resource bundles (pages 79–81).

- Collaborate with your team (pages 81–83).

· · · · · · · · · · · · · · · · · · ·

CHAPTER FOUR

Simplify How You Teach

I threw the party of the decade.

My girls' birthdays are just days apart, so we had this crazy idea to invite all three of their first-grade and kindergarten classes to one big swim party. I rented our community pool, and my idea seemed brilliant. Until . . . a massive storm blew in out of nowhere. We live near Phoenix. We almost never have storms. What are the odds that strong wind, rain, and lightning would make their way to our pool party?

We had no choice. We grabbed all the kids, food, and presents and moved the party to our house. We didn't have any entertainment or party games. The kids were supposed to be swimming! But what we did have was over forty sugar-crazed kids running (literally) around our house carrying pizza slices and fruit punch juice boxes. There is nothing that can prepare someone for this level of chaos. Nothing.

The next morning, walking around the house with a garbage bag, I felt like I was cleaning up from a frat party rather than a kid party. The weirdest thing is that my fish-shaped bathroom rug was missing. I grilled each of my kids. No one had any clue where the rug had gone. Who takes a bathroom rug from a kids' party? My answer came days later.

I was checking my mailbox at school. Imagine my surprise when I found my bathroom rug shoved into the small box. A note was attached that said something like:

"Mrs. Sears, I am so sorry we took your rug. My son pooped on it, so I brought it home to wash."

Now, have you ever thrown a party like that? In the Sears family, we go big!

Why am I telling you about our crazy party and poopy rug? As teachers, we tend to be drawn to chaos. Sometimes, this is our greatest asset. Other times, it causes us to make things more complicated than they need to be. Because we have to feel like we're doing the most all the time, we often create work for ourselves when something simple would do.

The result is overwhelm and exhaustion.

Falling in love with teaching again means simplifying some of our teaching strategies so that we can squelch some of that daily chaos and enjoy more lightbulb moments.

In this chapter, I'm going to show you some ways to change what's going on in your classroom. Some of these strategies and techniques might seem too good to be true right now. Like you, I've tried multiple "best ways" to optimize or make our teaching more effective and *quieter*... with absolutely disastrous results. Remember the time I planned a pool party for forty kids under the age of seven? Yep. Still me.

But here's the truth: in order to fulfill the definition of success you wrote out as your homework in chapter 1—you did that, right?—the way you teach *has* to change.

There's no way you can keep up with multiple separate small groups every day in centers or create a-ha moments for students when your classroom is in chaos. Let's keep you sane and your students learning by simplifying what you're doing in the classroom.

Strategy #1 • FOCUS ON CREATING RELATIONSHIPS.

When I was working at the Arizona Supreme Court, my boss was downright awful. He was quite a bit older than me and he was a lawyer. He looked down on young me with no experience and nothing more than a bachelor's degree. He would exclude me from office lunch invitations and he never asked me about myself or my family. When I got pregnant, he started to treat me even worse. Even though I had a high-level position as a lobbyist, he once called me into his office to refill his stapler. I couldn't help it. I told him where to shove it. When I worked for this man, I put in minimal effort. I did what I had to do, but nothing more. I was not motivated to be more valuable to him. No one wants to work hard, try new things, or be vulnerable with someone they don't know, like, and trust.

The same is true for students. They aren't willing to take risks, fail, or ask for help unless they feel safe and loved. When a student knows, likes, and trusts the teacher, they are willing to work harder and go the extra mile. When the relationship is strong, the lightbulb moments become more frequent. What this boils down to is that if you want to increase student achievement, you need to get to know your students—not just academically, but personally as well.

I am a proud introvert. (Seriously, I am a pro at coming up with excuses to get out of going to parties, showers, weddings, and concerts.) Having to be in a relationship with twenty-five-ish people at one time was terrifying to me. If I am to be really honest, I wasn't even sure how I was going to remember their names, much less their cat's name and their favorite flavor of ice cream. As a brand-new teacher I felt that I needed to learn it all on day one and then remember it forever more. But a relationship actually deepens with time. All year, you will be learning new and interesting tidbits about your students.

I'll never forget Sam. He was super short, but big on personality. Just a couple months into the school year, I noticed that his grades were slipping and he was less and less engaged in lessons. He was absent almost every Friday. This was proving to be especially tricky because we had more assessments on Fridays than on other days. He was always having to make these up the following week, which meant he was missing practice time. It had a domino effect. One day during snack time, I started a conversation with Sam.

"You have been absent the last several Fridays. We miss you when you are gone."

"I have to be gone on Fridays. That's the visiting day at the prison. It's the only time that I get to see my dad."

The conversation was like a sucker punch to my heart. No eight-year-old should have to deal with such big feelings, but unfortunately some do. After that conversation, I worked hard to find time to give Sam the Friday work and assessments ahead of time so that he wasn't always playing catch-up. He began to open up to me and we would have very regular chats during recess. He would tell me about missing his dad and that his mom worked a lot. His brother, who was only a few years older, would watch him most days. Sam trusted me with his thoughts and feelings.

Sam was never a straight-A student. But he grew more than any other kiddo in my class that year. The proud look on his face when I passed back graded papers made my day.

Several years later I ran into Sam's mom at the grocery store. She was excited to tell me about how Sam was doing in middle school. "I am so glad I ran into you. Sam is doing so well in school. You have always been his favorite teacher. He just felt such a connection to you. Thank you!"

The relationships you build with your students will have immediate and lasting results, just like my relationship with Sam.

Here are some simple strategies for building student relationships. None of these strategies take lots of classroom time or personal time.

TIP #1 • Connect with three students daily.

Set a goal to intentionally make a connection with three individual students each day. You can use a class checklist on your phone or assign the three students to each day in your lesson plans. It's important that you plan this out so that it doesn't get forgotten with the usual hustle and bustle of the classroom.

When you are intentionally looking to connect with a student, look for an opportunity to ask a nonacademic question. This can be done as the class is coming in during the morning, during a transition, during snack, at recess, or when the class is packing up. This should not feel like a formal meeting where the student is called to your desk. Instead it is just an informal and casual chat. The objective is to learn more about them as a person. Avoid yes-or-no questions and try to stick to open-ended questions that are more likely to lead to a back-and-forth conversation. Here are some question suggestions:

What did you have for breakfast today?
What are you doing after school?
What did you do over the weekend?
What are you looking forward to this weekend?

What have you been reading lately?

Tell me more about your shirt. Is that a band or a movie name?

After you ask the question, make sure you are actively listening to their response. Look them in the eyes and nod as they talk. Ask follow-up questions if there is time. Show them that you are interested in their life.

With every class I find that there are some students that are easy to connect with quickly, while others take much more time. That's totally normal! Don't become discouraged. In fact, when I have a student who is struggling with classroom behavior and expectations and connecting with myself and other students, I will intentionally use all three of my conversations for a day on the one student. Instead of putting three students on my list, I will focus on connecting with the one. I'll look for opportunities to talk to them in the morning, in the early afternoon, and just before release. These can be conversations about the same topic or three different topics. The important thing is that they are not academic conversations. We are not talking about homework, the math lesson, or their behavior in the school library. Instead, I am trying to learn more about their family, hobbies, routines, and likes and dislikes outside school. I find that if I do this for a few days, I see a huge difference in their classroom behavior. You can't expect perfection, but you will see progress.

TIP #2 • Send home positive notes.

Some parents are accustomed to hearing from the classroom teacher only when there is a problem. I still hold my breath when I see an email or a phone call coming in from my teenagers' high school. When I started sending positive notes home, I really wanted to improve my relationship with parents and guardians. That definitely happened. I started to get beautiful emails thanking me for taking the time to write the note. But something even bigger happened. Students beamed with pride when I gave them the note to take home to their adult. They knew that I was proud of them and that I noticed and heard them. They felt loved!

Sending notes home can become such a time-consuming task, though. It's important to find ways to simplify the routine or it will be difficult to stay consistent. I bought a huge stack of notecards from Target and kept them right next to my lesson plan binder. Every week, when I added my new lesson plans to the binder, I would stick five notecards, one for each day, in the binder pocket. During pack up, I would write two to three sentences on one card and hand it to the appropriate student to take home. I didn't write a lengthy letter. A couple sentences did the trick. After I wrote the card, I would check the student off the class list I kept in the binder. I tried to send a note with every student once every four to five weeks.

Another way to use positive notes is to keep a stack of sticky notes close by. Look for one student each day who has been extra awesome or one student who needs a pick-me-up. Write a quick sentence on the sticky note and leave it on their desk. Just one quick note per day can mean the world to a kiddo.

Strategy #2 • SPEND MORE TIME TEACHING PROCEDURES.

I am going to out myself with this embarrassing story. If nothing else, this story will help remind you of your awesomeness as a teacher. So here goes . . .

I did my student teaching in a high school government classroom. I really thought I might like to teach high school students—until I actually spent time in a high school classroom. (Bless you, high school teachers! You really are heroes.) I ended up taking more tests and eventually found a job teaching third grade. I had never started the year with third graders, only high schoolers. I did the only thing I knew how to do and wrote a five-page, single-spaced syllabus. This lengthy document included all classroom rules, expectations, procedures, and policies. It was the most boring thing I have ever written. But that's not all. Do you know what I did with this horrid document?

I sat my students at their desks and spent the first two days of school going line by line through the syllabus with them. I suspect every one of my students went home and told their parents just how boring I was and how much they wished they could be in a different class where they would have more fun.

See, you are already a million times better a teacher than I was! I have never heard of another elementary teacher creating a high-school-level syllabus for her students.

Besides building relationships, teaching your students procedures (how our classroom will be run) is the most important thing we can do with our class time at the beginning of the year—and anytime students need a refresher. Academic achievement increases when students feel confident about expectations. We all know this, and yet we often rush through this part because of the pressure we feel to teach every standard to mastery before the big test.

Here is the ugly truth: if we have to stop to lecture our students about behavior multiple times per day for the entire school year, we lose a significant amount of teaching time. It will make it harder and harder to squeeze all of those standards in. It also will decrease the aha moments we get to witness.

In contrast, if we invest more time up front into teaching the procedures, we will spend less time on classroom management throughout the year. This means more time to teach, less stress on a daily basis, and more joy in your whole career.

If you feel like you just don't know how to teach procedures, you're not alone! A lot of teachers feel like they have no clue. No one *wants* to be the boring syllabus teacher! (Trust me. I threw away the syllabus before my second year of teaching.)

Teachers have an amazing gift for being able to make just about anything into a fun activity—including procedures.

But just in case you are coming up blank right now, I have a few ideas.

TIP #1 • Model what *not* to do.

Showing students how to line up for lunch or pack up at the end of the day is all fine and good. But you can ramp up the fun (and the retention) by having students model what *not* to do. An example my students always loved was a lesson about the procedures for borrowing a book from the classroom library.

First, my students learned when they could go to the classroom library, how many books they could borrow, and how to return the books.

Then I would choose a student to demonstrate how *not* to use the classroom library. He might run to the library while talking. Then he might take two different books off the shelves and leave a few on the floor or in the wrong box. He might talk the entire time.

After a while, I would call him back to the floor and the class would talk about the things he did that were not allowed. Finally, I would ask him to model exactly how to use the classroom library correctly.

Whenever I taught procedures this way, there was always lots of laughter. This is fun and enjoyable on its own, and did you know that laughter actually releases chemicals into the brain that help to increase memory?* True story! Just make sure that after your class has a blast showing you how to complete a procedure wrong, you ask them to model the correct behavior.

---

*Sarah Henderson, "Laughter and Learning: Humor Boosts Retention," *Edutopia*, March 31, 2015, https://www.edutopia.org/blog/laughter-learning-humor-boosts-retention-sarah-henderson.

TIP #2 • Make procedures into a game.

There are so many simple ways to turn procedure practice into a game. My favorite is to write a series of questions about your classroom procedures on index cards. These can be questions like:

> *What do you do if you have to use the restroom while Mrs. Sears is teaching?*
> *What do you do if your pencil breaks during centers?*
> *Where can you find extra glue sticks?*

Pair these questions with a board game that most of your students already know how to play. I love to use Candy Land or tic-tac-toe. To earn a turn, the student must first answer their procedure question correctly.

Using games to review procedures also gives students a chance to practice game playing and group-work procedures! It's a real win-win.

TIP #3 • Let the students do the teaching.

Split your students into small groups and give each group one procedure. Students should create a presentation using technology or anchor chart paper to teach their procedure to the class.

Regardless of how you choose to practice procedures, resist the urge to move on before your class is ready. Every group will take a different amount of time to be truly independent and understand all the classroom expectations. Be patient and remember that you are saving time and frustration later.

> ## Want more help with procedures?
>
> Check out a complete—and completely printable!—list of procedures to teach and practice in your classroom in our book resources at notsowimpyteacher.com/bookresources.

Strategy #3 • SIMPLIFY YOUR SYSTEMS.

There were days when I spent more time managing bathroom breaks, searching for missing glue caps, and breaking up arguments over who should take the attendance list to the office than I did teaching legitimate lessons. Or at least it felt that way.

There are undoubtedly a lot of systems to create and manage in the classroom. And the more complicated you make those systems, inevitably the more time and joy they will steal from your day. The more you simplify the systems, the less you will have to stress about them on a daily basis and the more time you will have to teach and students will have to learn. Simple systems make it a lot easier to love your job.

There are lots of systems you probably need to simplify in your classroom, but here are a few ideas I've used.

TIP #1 • Sharpen pencils in advance.

My first year of teaching, pencils were mistakenly left off my supply list. We did not have pencils all year. I was always begging parents for donations and then buying them myself. When I finally had pencils, I had to figure out who would sharpen them and what to do when a student lost their pencil.

I have tried all the nifty pencil management systems you can find on Pinterest. Who knew a pencil could cause so much stress? I mean, there should probably be an entire class in college about pencils. The pencil wars and class competitions just felt like way too much work for me and wasted far too much class time.

In the end, the simplest method was the best. I had a tin for sharp pencils and a tin for broken or dull pencils. One student sharpened the pencils at the end of every day. If a student needed a pencil, they could grab one from the tin. No questions asked. No checkout system. No class money needed. Just get a pencil and get back to work.

The simplicity was golden!

TIP #2 • Stop being the sheriff of bathroom breaks.

I was in Mrs. Little's fifth-grade class. We had just gotten back from recess when I realized that I needed to pee. Yup, I was *that* kid. I asked Mrs. Little if I could go to the bathroom, and she said, "No, you should have gone during recess."

She wasn't wrong. But I hadn't gone during recess, and I had to go *now*. So I peed my pants on Mrs. Little's fifth-grade classroom carpet.

It was so embarrassing. Fifth grade is *way* too late to be peeing your pants. I had to tie my cardigan around my waist as I made the walk of shame to the nurse's office, where my mom was called. I couldn't look Mrs. Little in the face for the rest of the year.

Luckily, I have a stronger bladder now. If I didn't, I would never have made it as a teacher. But this experience helped me create simple bathroom routines for my students that did not involve having to police when a student should or shouldn't have to pee. (Because sometimes, you've just gotta go!)

I taught my students the routine of using the restroom at the start of any recess. I found a five-minute time during the morning to take a whole-class bathroom break. Otherwise, students were allowed to go to the bathroom when they needed to, but the preference was to wait until Mrs. Sears was done talking.

Did some students take advantage of this freedom? Maybe. I chose to handle it on a case-by-case basis rather than forcing all my students to "hold it" when they really needed to go. Honestly, can you really listen, learn, and do your best work when you feel like your bladder is going to explode? I can't.

TIP #3 • Limit classroom jobs.

During my first two years teaching, I brainstormed enough jobs for every student in my classroom. I had an elaborate display on the wall and I would rotate the jobs every week. Well, every week that I actually remembered to rotate them. The truth is that the job board was a lot of work for me. And the students? They often forgot to do their job or couldn't remember how to do the job since working through the rotation took months.

After a couple years of telling myself that I needed to get better at the job rotations, I decided to simplify things. Instead of having twenty-five helpers every day, I realized it would be easier to have fewer cooks in the kitchen. Having just two helpers per day would be more effective. I put all of my students' names on cutouts and split them into two piles. I chose one name from each pile every day. These two students did any task I needed them to do during the day.

This certainly made class jobs less stressful and time-consuming for me.

I noticed another benefit too. When students had individual jobs, they would do something only if it was their job. For example, if a student saw a book on the floor, they would leave it there unless they were assigned to be the librarian that day.

With my new system, I taught students that taking care of the classroom was everyone's job. The helpers weren't there to clean up after everyone. Instead, their job was to help me by running errands or passing out papers. Therefore, if a student saw a book on the floor, they felt responsible, picked it up, and put it back where it belonged.

Strategy #4 • MAKE DIFFERENTIATING EASY AGAIN.

I was doing a live training recently with about 600 teachers. I was sharing some strategies for teaching students to compare fractions. I mentioned a few ways to differentiate these strategies for their learners. A teacher bravely asked, "Are you always differentiating?" Heck yeah! I'm always differentiating because all my students are at different levels and learn in different ways. When we meet students where they are, we increase their confidence and witness more of those lightbulb moments.

But differentiating can be hard. Like, really hard.

Maybe you were like me. I thought that differentiating meant giving different assignments and activities to students based on their level. I had four different reading groups and every group was doing something very different. When a student was struggling, I looked for a different activity especially for them. If students finished fast, I had a whole bucket of different activities for them. The planning, teaching, and grading of all of these activities was so overwhelming!

Let me drop a truth bomb . . .

Giving different assignments is not the only way to differentiate! It's one way. And honestly, it's probably the most complicated way. I am not saying you will never need to give a different assignment when differentiating, but I am saying it shouldn't be the only way you differentiate or even your go-to way to differentiate.

Simplify differentiation whenever possible! Here are a few ideas to get you started:

TIP #1 • Differentiate with supports.

An easy way to differentiate—and to help students have more of those lightbulb moments—is to provide supports or resources for those who need them. When your class is skip counting, you can display the numbers on the board. Those who need to look can and others can close their eyes. When the class is doing a grammar task-card scoot, allow some students to use their interactive notebooks during the activity. If your students are playing math games or completing center activities, allow students who need it to use their multiplication chart. This type of differentiation doesn't involve any extra planning or prep!

TIP #2 • Shorten the assignment.

I was at a training session hosted by the writers of our math curriculum. The trainer was talking about giving students no more than ten minutes to complete the practice sheet each day. A teacher said, "But lots of my students wouldn't be able to finish the sheet in just ten minutes." The trainer actually looked surprised. He said, "We never intended for every student to be able to complete the entire practice sheet each day." Mic drop.

Our math worksheet and most other worksheets out there start with the easier or more concrete problems. They gradually get more complex and abstract. Students who are above grade level will work through the problems very quickly and finish the worksheet in a short period of time. The on-level students will probably work through the first few problems quickly and slow down toward the end. They might finish about three-fourths of the problems in the same amount of time. Students who are struggling with the concept will probably work very slowly through the first few problems. They might be slowed down because of slower reading, drawing pictures to solve, or even using manipulatives. They will probably complete only half the worksheet. That's differentiation! The struggling students aren't ready for the more complex problems and the above-level students are being challenged.

You can differentiate by giving work time and focusing on accuracy instead of completion. You can also cross off half an assignment, or require that certain students complete only a fraction of the centers.

Strategy #5 • MAKE SMALL GROUPS AND CENTERS EASIER TO MANAGE.

The very best way to differentiate and meet the needs of the diverse learners in our classroom is with small groups. When I was a kid, my teacher delivered almost every lesson to the entire class. Every single student received exactly the same lesson.

In that approach, about a third of the students were bored because they were ready for more of a challenge. Another third of the class was completely lost because they weren't ready for this skill yet. And only a third were actually learning whatever skill the teacher was teaching that day.

Best practices in K–12 education have come a long way since I was in grade school. (Seriously, I am pretty old!) Most teachers know that small group instruction is ideal because it gives us the opportunity to meet every student where they are and gives us the opportunity to better understand a student's thinking.

However, in order to teach effectively to a segment of the class in each small group, we need the rest of the class to be engaged in their center activities. And holy heck, center time can be the epitome of classroom chaos! I remember what my students said like it was yesterday.

"Mrs. Sears, I'm done. What do I do now?"

"Can I go to the bathroom?"

"Alex licked my shoe and he won't say sorry!"

"My Chromebook won't work."

"I don't get it."

"When is it going to be lunch time?"

Besides the nonstop interruptions, you are trying to squeeze a lot of intense teaching into a small block of time. As soon as you start reading with the group or you get one math problem solved, you need to switch groups, which often includes making the students move from table to table.

Small-group time can be chaotic. Don't even get me started on the talking and the overall classroom noise level. You could have students arguing over a game and students talking about the kickball match that will be happening at recess while the quietest student in your whole class is trying to ask you a question about math.

It's no wonder that you feel thoroughly exhausted at the end of small-group or center time. It doesn't surprise me one bit that teachers start to cancel this part of their day. Who wants all that crazy on a daily basis?

But what if I told you that small-group and center time can be easier? And that it's possible to enjoy this time more and make the time you teach each group more effective and lasting, as well as make your students more independent learners? I know. It sounds too good to be true, right? I promise it's not.

One Not So Wimpy Teacher, Candra, used this method to simplify her classroom and save her tons of energy. During her first year of teaching, she had three groups each day and she struggled to meet all the needs of all her students. Transitioning (especially with first graders) was taking too much valuable time. She thought she was expected to meet with each student every day, so she did.

During her second year, she figured she could meet her students' needs better with four groups. Four groups in one day seemed like a hot mess, so she decided to split it up. She met with two groups each day and it made a world of difference. Her transitions were quicker and smoother. Plus, her students got more out of their centers, especially teacher table, and it made prep work a lot easier. After that, she never went back to her old ways. She even converted her neighbor teacher to this style of center rotations as she saw how well centers were going in her classroom.

As teachers, we've gotten used to the craziness because we feel like we *have* to meet with every single student in our classroom every day. It's a *must*. And because of that, some kids are *always* going to be off task and transitions *cannot* be fluid or easy.

Am I right?

Actually, no, I am not right.

In reality, it's totally possible to have centers and small-group time that's organized and relatively peaceful, where the noise and energy level is at a seven instead of a ten or eleven. The chaos a lot of us experience on a daily basis seems normal only because everyone else is experiencing it too.

My point is that just because something feels normal doesn't mean it is. If you're one of those teachers who thinks you can't do centers because your kids are too wound up and misbehaved, listen up. The next four tips will make small-group and center time not just possible, but less stressful, more impactful, and way more fun.

TIP #1 • Stop meeting with four or more groups every day.

I don't know where this practice started, but when I work with teachers, they almost always have four reading or math groups and try to meet with each every day. One teacher I talked to reported having *nine groups*. Nine!

On paper, splitting your students into distinct groups based on their skill level can sound like a good idea. Perhaps you have an hour for small groups. If you've got a reasonable four groups—like most teachers—then you might plan to spend fifteen minutes a day with each group. That way, each student will receive small-group instruction daily. Awesome, right?

Wrong. This isn't reality. Within that structure, you're forgetting to include time for five different transitions between groups. If every transition is three minutes long, you have already lost fifteen minutes of your small-group time. Now you have only eleven minutes with each group. Once you give them materials and instructions, how much time will they really have to read or solve a math problem? It gets very tight! And quite honestly, moving between that many groups of kids is exhausting. This is when you start to feel like you are running a marathon. (Or hosting a party with forty-plus seven-year-olds!)

There is a simple solution. It might sound crazy at first, but hear me out with an open mind. Split your class into four leveled groups. *And meet with only two groups per day.*

I know. But give me a chance to explain.

Meeting with fewer groups means you will have fewer transitions and more time to work with the students in these groups. The longer work time will make it possible to dig deeper into the text or complete more math problems using manipulatives. The longer chunk of time also helps students make more progress and allows your small-group time to be less crunched and therefore less chaotic.

You might be thinking, "But what about my struggling students who need small-group time every day?"

I got you. When I switched to meeting with two groups per day, I found that I was actually spending more time per week with each student than when I met with four groups every day. And I can prove it to you—no manipulatives needed.

In my classroom, I started out spending one hour in small group four days a week. When I met with four groups per day, I had to rotate groups every fifteen minutes. But that didn't mean I actually spent fifteen minutes with each student—because of transition time. Even if I am generous and say that my students could effectively transition in four minutes each and every time, that meant I spent eleven minutes with each group per day. That, as you can see in the table below, meant I spent roughly forty-four minutes each week with each group or child. And that was if everything went right and there were no crayon thieves, contagious giggles, or the usual antics of third graders left to supervise themselves.

Compare that forty-four minutes per week to the fifty-two minutes per week I got to spend when I met with only two groups per day. Sure, the students saw me less often—only two days a week—but each time they got twenty-six minutes with me instead of eleven. Plus, with fewer transitions come fewer hijinks and potential distractions. The math is simple and listed below. Keep in mind that this table also takes into consideration the time needed to transition between groups.

Four Groups Per Day =	Two Groups Per Day =
15 minute rotations minus 4 minutes for transitions	30 minute rotations minus 4 minutes for transitions
11 minutes x 4 =	**26 x 2 =**
44 minutes per week	52 minutes per week

In general, meeting with just two groups per day for longer stretches of time, with fewer transitions needed, meant that I actually spent more small-group minutes each week with all my learners.

The next question I know is coming from you is: "But I have to do a lesson every day or I will never make it through the curriculum before the end of the year."

I get that! I taught a new lesson every day. There is no need to slow down the pace of your whole group lessons. The reality is that you are going to have more than twice as much time with a small group. You can go over a problem from yesterday's lesson and one from today's lesson depending on the needs of the students in the group.

TIP #2 • Stop changing your center activities every week.

When I first started to use centers, I was always looking for new activities to entertain my students. I thought new and exciting activities would keep them engaged and make it easier for me to meet with my small groups. In essence, I wanted the activities to be babysitters. So I was always searching Pinterest and Teachers Pay

Teachers for cheap or free games and activities every week. I was especially attracted to the cute seasonal ones because I was certain my students would love them. Every week I was cutting, gluing, labeling, and laminating new centers. Then I had to devote class time every Monday to teach my students how to complete the new center activities. The result? I wasted a *ton* of time and my students never felt confident with the center activities, which led to a lack of independence and understanding. Well, yikes. That wasn't the plan!

My first mistake was treating centers like entertainment for my students. When all is said and done, students will spend a significant amount of class time in centers each week. We need that to be valuable time. Therefore, centers should be a review of the skills we are teaching the whole group and reinforcing within each small group. The activities can be fun, but also need to have a purpose.

The second mistake that I made was setting my students up for failure by constantly changing out the center activities. I didn't want them to get bored, but what I failed to realize is that I was making it almost impossible for them to feel confident with the directions and expectations of the activities. Trying to do something new and exciting constantly actually caused some of my students to become very anxious!

The solution is to find a few center activities that can stay the same all year. You may be switching the skill out every few weeks, but the actual activity should remain the same. Now you can spend time teaching the expectations, and students will have the tools to be successful all year. This significantly increases their independence. Their focus is now on the skill rather than on the directions for completing the activity.

Keeping the centers the same all year is going to save you some serious time as well! You will invest some time up front to find activities that can be used all year, but then you won't have to go on wild goose chases on Pinterest every week going forward.

Here are some ideas to get you thinking about activities that can be used all year:

Reading Centers	Math Centers
Read to self	Math fact games
Respond to reading prompts	Bundle of math centers for every skill
Student magazines	Math journal prompts
Apps or websites	Apps or websites

TIP #3 • Stop making small-group activities complicated.

When I first started doing small groups for reading and math, I was killing myself writing elaborate lesson plans for every single small group. Each group was doing different activities that I had to prepare. It was a whole lot like planning and preparing for four different classes. It wore me out fast! It didn't take me long to realize that I needed to simplify things. You don't need complicated activities in order to differentiate your small groups.

> "I had ten different stations and I changed them all out every Friday!"
>
> –Krysten

What would you do with your small-group time if it were easy?

I decided every reading group would do book clubs. We would choral read together for two-thirds of the time and then fill in a graphic organizer about what we read. I did this with all my groups, which made planning easy. I was also able to make differentiation simple. Every group read a different book based on their reading level. We would read the book at the group's pace so there was no need to stress about finishing the book at the same time as any other group. I also differentiated the graphic organizer. Every group used the same organizer, but in different ways. Some groups did it independently. Other groups worked with a partner. My lowest group filled out the organizer with lots of my support.

My math groups were just as simple to plan and prep for. The small-group time was used to practice the skills I had taught to the entire class. I would choose problems from the practice or homework sheet for students to solve. Some groups used lots of manipulatives. Some groups were ready to do the problems with limited manipulatives and more drawing. We would work at the group's pace and I would offer the support that was needed based on their level. These problems were all done on whiteboards and so I almost never had to prep anything special for my small groups. (If you want to take the chaos out of your math centers, check out The Not So Wimpy Masterclass at notsowimpyteacher.com/awesome.)

Strategy #6 • SIMPLIFY FAST-FINISHER ACTIVITIES.

All your students do not work at the same pace. It's a fact, and it can be a pain because we always need to come up with fast-finisher activities for those students who work at a faster pace. Even more stuff to prep! Ugh! A lot of the teachers I know want these activities to be a valuable use of time, but we also don't want to make the activities so good that students rush (and undoubtedly make silly errors) so they can work on a super-fun fast-finisher project.

Like a lot of things in teaching, fast-finisher activities can be a balancing act that feels impossible to win.

I am kind of embarrassed to admit this, but I already told you about my poop rug, so what do I really have to lose? I used to spend hours and hours every single week making photocopies of math-fact printables for my fast finishers. I can actually remember being at the school for my son's orchestra concert, running to the copy room between performances to add more paper to the copier. Reams and reams of paper later and all I had were a few papercuts, an annoyed husband, and a boring activity for my math fast finishers. What was I thinking?

After trying just about everything, I came to the realization that once again, simplicity is the answer! (It almost always is. Why can't I remember that when I am making everything complicated?)

Here is what my fast finishers would do:

Reading: Read to themselves or visit the class library
Writing: Write a new story
Math: Practice math facts

Super simple, right? There are two things I want to point out. First, none of these activities require prep on my part. No more late nights in front of the copy machine. Also, none of these activities need to be turned in and graded. Fast-finisher work is just extra practice for my students, not extra work for me!

Strategy #7 • FALL IN LOVE WITH YOUR *LEAST* FAVORITE SUBJECT.

Math was my favorite subject to teach. I loved how hands-on math can be, and I loved teaching a variety of strategies so that students could experiment until they found the strategy that worked best for them. When I was prepping, I always spent significantly more time looking up math games, activities, and strategies than I did for other subjects. I would excitedly try new math routines in my quest to make math lessons more hands-on and help my students gain a deeper understanding of concepts. I loved growing as a math educator. It was like I was getting a dopamine hit every time I thought about making math even more effective in my classroom.

On the other hand, I hated teaching writing. I thought I was going to be an amazing writing teacher because I have always enjoyed writing myself. As a child I wanted to be an author. I used to check out the thesaurus from the school library and sit on the wall at recess writing stories with super-interesting word choices.

When I became a teacher, I just assumed that students would love writing as much as I do. That couldn't have been further from reality. My students hated to write. They had zero confidence, zero stamina, and zero desire. As I stared into the eyes of my bored and miserable writers, I realized that I lacked skills and strategies to effectively teach writing.

If you are like me and want to learn how to confidently teach writing, check out the Not So Wimpy Teacher writing masterclass at notsowimpyteacher.com/yes.

Like a lot of teachers, I never had a class in college that was devoted to teaching writing. Liking to write is just not the same as knowing how to teach it. So I started to hate writing time. I hated preparing for the lessons. I spent very little time learning new strategies or looking for resources. Instead, I just prayed that math would go long so that I had an excuse to skip writing. Heck, I even hoped for a fire drill during writing time. Standing outside in the heat with twenty-five eight-year-olds sounded better than teaching writing.

If you have ever found yourself hating one subject (or at least strongly disliking it), then you know how quickly that negativity can steal the joy of teaching. It's hard to love teaching if you dread a certain time of day every day. If you want to love teaching again, it makes sense to find a way to love (or at least like) your least favorite subject. But how?

Think about your very favorite subject. One of the reasons you probably enjoy teaching this subject is that you are getting results. So ask yourself these questions:

"What am I doing in that subject that is working?"

"Can I use similar strategies with my least favorite subject?"

They are simple questions, but the answers can make all the difference. When it came to falling in love with writing, I asked myself, what am I doing in my favorite subject—math—that is working? Here are some answers I brainstormed:

- Teaching in units of study to allow students to master a unit before moving on
- Breaking skills into small pieces and scaffolding them into lessons
- Giving students opportunities to practice new skills immediately
- Offering choice
- Meeting with small groups
- Using manipulatives

The list was longer, but you get the gist. Then I asked, can I use any of these strategies when I teach writing? The answer was a big ol' heck yes!

First I started to teach writing in longer units of study like I was doing in math.

Instead of jumping around from one genre to the next, we started to spend an entire eight weeks on each genre.

Next I realized that I was trying to teach my students *everything* good writers do all in one lesson. I decided to break these lessons into much smaller pieces so that I could scaffold the lessons.

Then I started letting my writers choose their writing utensil and the topic of their writing rather than requiring #2 yellow pencils and giving a mandated prompt.

And instead of trying to meet with students one-on-one to look at their writing, I created small conference groups so that I could meet with students more often.

Each of these changes helped my students be more successful. They started to enjoy writing more, which led to noticeable growth. When my students enjoyed writing and were getting results, I started to like to teach writing too! While writing never replaced math as my favorite subject to teach, I stopped dreading my writing workshop time. Teaching writing no longer stole my joy on a daily basis, and every once in a while I even caught myself having fun.

Strategy #8 • MAKE IT FUN, BUT KEEP IT SIMPLE.

Making learning fun was so important to me that I often found myself doing crazy activities that cost a fortune and took tons of time to prepare. I did book tastings, room transformations, themed parties, elaborate art projects, and guest speakers. The students usually had fun, and I loved to see them having fun. But sometimes I would go home so worn out that I couldn't enjoy my family. Sometimes I would get so carried away with creating the fun that I would lose track of the standards and the learning targets. Other times I would get stressed out about the cost of the supplies.

Having fun and seeing your students have fun helps keep the teaching love alive. So I am certainly not suggesting that you never do any big parties or room transformations. I am, however, suggesting that you choose wisely and limit them to what feels fun and manageable for you.

The good news is that you can easily add fun to your everyday classroom without turning your classroom into an operating room or even getting out the glitter. Having fun while keeping it simple will help decrease the overwhelm. Here are some easy ideas:

TIP #1 • Provide lots of opportunities for choice.

Do you remember those Choose Your Own Adventure books from your tween years? They were the best because you actually got to direct how the story would unfold. Choice is amazing! Everything is more fun when you have choices. Going out to eat is exciting because you can order anything you want from the menu— even if it's a meal your spouse and children would never eat. Our televisions now have about 1,000 channels, and as if that is not enough, we can stream shows on a number of different apps. You can choose to watch almost any show or movie from the comfort of your home whenever you feel like it.

Adding choice to the classroom can be very easy. It definitely does not mean creating a bunch of different assignments and letting students choose which one to work on. No way. That's too much work! Here are some simple ways to offer choice to your students:

- Choosing their own topics for their writing rather than working from a prompt
- Choosing the order of center activities

- Choosing places in the classroom to complete centers, writing, or an independent assignment
- Choosing their own partners
- Choosing a game to play from a small assortment
- Choosing their own books for independent reading time

TIP #2 • Turn boring worksheets into simple games.

The key here is to keep it super simple! Students don't need elaborate games to have fun. A simple game can be far more fun than the usual worksheet. I love to replace worksheets with interactive notebooks, task cards, and centers, but sometimes a worksheet is necessary. Sometimes a worksheet is just easy. But you can still make it fun. You don't have to make a worksheet into a game every day, but sprinkle some games in from time to time and your students will be all smiles. Below are a couple of game ideas that can be used for any subject. (Want a handout to remind you? Visit notsowimpyteacher.com/bookresources.)

Roll Your Score

Students work with a partner and take turns to complete questions or problems from a worksheet. When a student completes the question, the partner checks their work. If it is accurate, the student rolls two dice and adds them together. The number represents the points that the student earns for that problem. Now it is their partner's turn to work on the next question. Students will go back and forth until all the questions are answered. Then they add up their points to see who scored the highest.

Connect Four

This is a great game to play with table groups. Assign each group a color of sticky notes. Draw a grid on your whiteboard. Groups must work together to solve a problem on their worksheet. If their answer is accurate, they can put one of their team's sticky notes on the grid. When a problem is solved, the group moves on to another problem and repeats the process. The first team to get four of their sticky notes in a row on the grid is the winning team.

Random Numbers

Students can work independently for this game. Display a hundreds chart on your white board. Students will work to complete questions on their worksheet. Once a student has completed one (or more, if you want), they come to you to have their answer checked. If it is accurate, they can write their name in one box on the hundreds chart. When you run out of time, use a random number generator app to pick a few numbers. If a student's name is on that number they earn a prize or reward.

TIP #3 • Get students up and moving.

Allowing your students to get up from their desks and move on a regular basis helps increase their focus and decrease fidgeting. And it's so fun!

Task-Card Scoot

Task-card scoots were always a fan favorite in my classroom and so I made a point to include at least one scoot per week. Spread the cards around the classroom and give students a recording sheet. Students start with the card closest to them and then move around the room answering the questions on each of the task cards. To keep it simple, I do not set a timer and require students to move to the next card when the timer goes off. Some kids need longer, and some kids are done quicker. I let students work at their own pace to help keep them on task and decrease the pressure.

Brain Breaks

Brain breaks are great transition activities that help students refocus before moving to the next activity. They are a simple way to add movement and fun to the classroom. I especially love to use brain breaks after recess, lunch, and specials. These are the times when it can be the toughest to get our students to focus. A brain break can be some stretching, some yoga moves, a simple chant, or even some free dancing.

HAVE MORE LIGHTBULB MOMENTS

It is so darn hot here in Phoenix. Half the days per year are 100 degrees or higher. You can easily cook an egg on the sidewalk during the summer. (But yuck! Don't eat sidewalk eggs!) And don't go off about it being a dry heat. Hot is hot.

Air-conditioning is a steep bill in Phoenix. My school would try to save some money over the summer by turning the AC temperature up to 90 degrees. The air would not come on until the room temperature hit the 90-degree mark. That is not a comfy room temperature. Since teachers have the entire summer off, this is no big deal, though, right? Not for me! I did not have any work and life balance in my early years of teaching, so I spent a good portion of every summer working in my classroom. But it was so hot that I was sweating more than working.

Until I had a literal lightbulb moment. I turned on a desk lamp and put the bulb right up to the thermostat in my classroom. As the lamp got hotter and hotter, the temperature on the thermostat started to rise. After it passed the 90-degree mark, the air-conditioning kicked on. Hallelujah! I had cool air blowing in my little room! And the best part? The AC stayed on the entire time I kept the lamp on because I fooled the thermostat into believing it was above 90 degrees.

Brilliant, right?

Classrooms are full of lightbulb moments (even if most of them don't involve an actual lightbulb). Teachers live for those moments when a student excitedly announces, "I get it now!" It's in those moments that we really feel like we are making a difference. And that's why we became teachers in the first place—to make a difference.

But let's be clear. Student achievement is not the measure of your own success! Student reading levels and standardized test scores are no longer a part of your definition of success. You wrote a new definition and included things you have control of. We already know that even the greatest teachers will have students who struggle to meet academic goals.

That being said, I also know that student success and those lightbulb moments are why you love teaching. I asked my teacher community what they loved most about teaching and 75 percent of the responses were something like, "The aha moments!" You love seeing your students learn and grow. I'm not surprised. It's not the definition of success, but it is still a key to loving teaching even more. The more lightbulb moments that happen in your classroom, the more you are going to love what you do.

There are many simple ways you can increase student achievement without adding more to your plate. When it comes to the actual *act* of teaching, simplicity is key. Keeping things simple helps your students be more confident and successful.

Keeping things simple also allows you to save time and decreases your overall stress.

So keep asking yourself, "How can I make ____ easier to implement and manage?"

. . . .

If you have time to do only one thing from this chapter, I want you to:

Spend more time teaching procedures.

Even if you are reading this halfway through the school year, spending time on procedures will prove to be valuable. If students cannot independently complete tasks, you will waste time with reminders and discipline. You'll go home happier every day when you know you are spending more time teaching multiplication strategies and the main idea than yelling, "We don't run in the classroom!"

. . . .

The Not So Wimpy Way to Simplify How You Teach

1. Focus on creating relationships (pages 89–93).

2. Spend more time teaching procedures (pages 93–97).

3. Simplify your systems (pages 97–100).

4. Make differentiating easy again (pages 100–102).

5. Make small groups and centers easier to manage (pages 102–110).

6. Simplify fast-finisher activities (pages 110–111).

7. Fall in love with your *least* favorite subject (pages 112–114).

8. Make it fun, but keep it simple (pages 114–119).

CHAPTER FIVE

Grading

have bitten only one dental hygienist. But apparently one is too many.

When I moved to a new town several years ago, I had to find a new dentist. This made me very nervous since I had been seeing my childhood dentist up until then. I got a referral from a friend and was instantly sold. It felt more like a spa than a dental office. I got to pick a movie to watch while they cleaned my teeth and I could even get a hand or neck massage afterward. This felt like a luxury for a mom of four young children. For a short period of time I actually thought that maybe I could start to enjoy my dentist appointments.

Then it happened. I was watching an Adam Sandler movie while the hygienist was shoving her whole hand in my mouth. Suddenly I felt like I was going to gag, and without thinking, I grabbed her hand. She was a little bit surprised but not angry. Before she continued cleaning my teeth, she put pot holders on my hands. I kid you not—pot holders! She said they would keep me from involuntarily grabbing her because it would make me more aware of my hand movement.

The pot holders did their job, because I did not grab her hands again . . . but moments later, I chomped down on her finger when she poked my gums. I swear to this day that I didn't do it intentionally! The pain just caught me off guard and I bit. Hard. I apologized profusely, but the hygienist looked very put out at this point.

Long story short, I received a call from the office later that day, stating that I needed to find a new dentist. No more movies and massages. No more pot holders.

One bite and I wasn't welcomed back.

If there was a list titled Crappy Things We Have to Do as Humans, I'd put going to the dentist pretty darn close to the top. (Going to funerals, eating vegetables, and getting pap smears would also be on that list.) Similarly, there are crappy things we have to do because we are teachers. A few things I would put on that list are being broke, saying goodbye to your students at the end of every year, and grading a million papers every single week. Ugh, grading. It's like going to the dentist—you always have to do it, and you know it serves a purpose, but . . . ugh.

I remember sitting in my high school English class and listening to my teacher complain about how much grading she needed to do and how it was going to take all weekend. I had just turned in a research paper that had taken me a month to complete. I felt disgusted by her complaints. I thought, "If you don't like grading so much, stop assigning us so much work to do." Oh, to go back to my teenage days, when the answers seemed so simple. The sad reality is that as teachers we have to assign and grade work.

Even if it's not our favorite part of the job, it is a necessity.

It's okay to love teaching and not love the grading. Heck, it's okay to hate grading. I sure did.

I love to scrapbook, but I hate having to put away all the paper scraps, markers, and stamps when I am finished.

I love being a mom, but potty training is the absolute pits.

I love to travel to new places, but I do not like sitting in those tiny airplane seats, especially when the person in front of me decides to recline theirs.

The point is that there is typically a downside to any job, hobby, or task.

But since most of us want to continue enjoying these activities, we look for ways to minimize the negative. I came up with a good organizational system to make cleaning up after my scrapbook projects a tad easier. I took an online course on potty training so that I could be just a bit more successful. When I travel, I make sure to download an entire season of a show I enjoy to help make the time on the plane pass faster.

And when it came to grading, I chose new strategies that decreased the amount of time I spent grading papers. I couldn't eliminate it altogether, but I certainly didn't need to spend every night and weekend cuddled up with a stack of papers to score. And neither do you.

As I was sitting down to write this exact chapter, I was procrastinating by scrolling through my social media. I happened to see a post with tips to help teachers get their grading done at school. The tips in the article weren't bad, but maybe a tad basic. The most interesting thing to me was the comments on the post. There were dozens of comments from teachers of all grade levels and almost every teacher was critical of the concept that you could avoid grading at home.

"This is so unrealistic! If I didn't bring papers home, how would I even get the grading done?"

"There is no way I can get my grading done during my forty-five-minute prep period!"

"I have fifty students. Grading takes a ton of time!"

Before I saw that, I was just going to fill these pages with the grading strategies that helped me to get my grading done in a fraction of the time, but it became obvious that none of these strategies will help if you don't believe that grading doesn't have to take up all your personal time. If you don't believe it is possible, your brain will offer up an argument about every one of these strategies. You'll think something like, "That will never work for me because . . ."

Can I be blunt? I hope you are giving me a big nod, because here it goes . . . sometimes our brains are jerks. Our brains convince us that our situations are super-duper unique. We are so different from everyone else, in fact, that even though these strategies have worked for countless other people, they will never work for us. That's how our brains get to win. Our brains can also rob us of the opportunity of trying new things or problem-solving to make a strategy work in our situation. Now, don't get too mad at your brain. It is not purposely trying to sabotage you. The truth is that your brain is trying to keep you safe. Trying new strategies is scary. Your brain is trying to protect you from potential failure. Unfortunately, in the process of protecting you, your brain ends up hurting you. You keep doing things exactly as you always have, and this leads to the exact same outcome you've always gotten. In our case, we keep bringing home huge stacks of papers to grade, which leads to stress and less enjoyable time to do what we want on weeknights and weekends.

The good news is that you can easily train your brain to be a problem solver rather than a scaredy cat. Anytime you hear your brain saying any form of, "This won't work for me," I want you to grab a sheet of paper and write this heading at the top: "How can I make this work for me?" Try brainstorming some solutions to those arguments your brain is presenting.

At first, you'll probably have nothing. You'll be like a third grader when you tell them it's time to write a story. You might stare at the clock, doodle a little bit, and think, "Do I have to write in complete sentences?" And when you find yourself acting like a third grader (minus picking your nose), you might need to take a break. I like to go for a walk, take a shower, or relax on the patio. The answer always comes if I keep repeating the question in my head.

All that said, I can't promise that every single strategy that I am about to share will work for you. (After all, sometimes admin will say "No way.") But I can promise that implementing even a few of these ideas will cut down your at-home grading time significantly.

I mean, it's worth a shot. Because won't it be easier to love teaching when you stop spending every free moment poring over essays and math tests? Heck yeah!

Strategy #1 • STOP GRADING EVERYTHING.

Every single activity you assign does not need to make it to the gradebook. Seriously, go back and reread that last sentence. This is a tough one for many of us, me included. The thought is that if we don't give a grade, students won't be motivated to complete the work. Or maybe you worry that not giving a grade on an activity means that you and your students wasted time completing the activity.

The truth is that it is perfectly fine to assign work so that students have the opportunity to practice new skills. Every assignment really shouldn't be assessed with a grade. In many cases, students aren't ready to be graded. I was guilty of this. I would teach my students a quick lesson on plural nouns and then give them a worksheet, which I graded, on the same skill. I was basically testing their understanding before ever giving them a chance to practice. Often, when you give students time to practice without the fear of failure and take fewer grades, you end up with higher scores!

Teachers in our Not So Wimpy community often ask us how many grades they should take for each subject each week. In true teacher fashion, I like to answer with another question. How many grades are you required to take each week? This is no time to be an overachiever. If your school is requiring two reading grades per week, then stick with two. Not three or four.

If your admin does not have a minimum number of grades requirement, here is my suggestion:

Reading: 1
Writing/Grammar/Spelling: 2
Math: 1
Science/Social Studies: 1

Another option is to take no more than three to five grades per week without breaking it down by subject. Sometimes you are just starting a new unit in science, or maybe you are spending the week doing research in writing. It just doesn't make sense to take a grade. Other weeks, there are multiple opportunities for students to show what they know in a particular subject.

The important lesson is that you need to give yourself permission to grade fewer assignments. This will decrease your workload and stress and can potentially improve the quality of your students' grades. As you are doing your lesson planning each week, highlight the assignments that will be graded. The rest of the work you can give a quick scan to check for understanding before dropping them in the recycle bin.

Strategy #2 • USE MORE INFORMAL ASSESSMENTS.

In the process of making answer keys, finding the perfect pen, and stressing about the huge stack of papers that need to be graded, we often forget the true reason that we are assessing our students.

It is not to get enough grades for the report card.

It is not to hold students accountable.

It is not because we need to prove something to parents.

We assess our students so that we can check for understanding. If they understand, we can move on. If they do not understand, we will reteach.

The great news is that checking for understanding does not always require a quiz, test, or worksheet that you will need to grade. You can easily check for understanding using simple informal assessments. These assessments may not appear as a letter grade on the report card, but they do provide key information you can use when planning future lessons.

Here are some informal assessment ideas:

- Exit tickets
- Ask students to answer a question and hold up their whiteboard
- Listening or watching students work during small groups
- Playing games
- Spot-checking an assignment while students are working

These informal assessments give you the opportunity to check for understanding before you give a more formal and graded assignment. You'll know if students need more support before you spend a lot of time grading assessments that leave you feeling disappointed by student performance.

Teachers Share Their Favorite Informal Assessments

"When I'm teaching I'll periodically have the kids hold up four, three, two, or one fingers to their chest. Four fingers means I got this and can help teach my classmates; three is I can do this by myself; two—I still need help, and one—Ms. B, I have no idea what you're talking about."

—Justine B.

"I love allowing my kids to work out a math problem on their desk with a dry-erase marker. I can easily walk around and see who gets it and who doesn't. I can also easily give another problem or add comments."

—Christina P.

"The first group I meet with during independent work time are those students who believe they need help. This allows me to see any gaps and address them quickly. By the time I am done with that group, other students have done enough work that I can quickly check in with them and reteach as necessary."

—Stacey F.

Strategy #3 • DON'T GRADE (OR GIVE) HOMEWORK.

I graded homework for the longest time. I sent home a packet of math sheets every week and then spent the weekend grading every single problem. I felt obligated to do so. I think I thought it was the only way I would know if students understood a skill (which is kind of ridiculous, now that I think about it). I also thought that parents would expect the assignment to be graded. And if I didn't grade homework, how would I be able to convince kids to actually complete the assignment? Plus, isn't homework supposed to help teach responsibility? I wish someone wiser had given me a reality check back in those early years. It would have saved me so many tears from stress and hours spent grading.

Before we tackle grading homework, it's important that we discuss the very act of assigning homework. I'm going to warn you that I feel passionate about this topic and I know my stance is controversial. With every fiber of my being, I believe we need to stop giving students homework. Yup, I said it. No homework—not just on the weekends, but every day.

Reasons to Stop Giving Homework

There is actually a huge movement in the United States among teachers, parents, and mental health experts to decrease and even eliminate homework. In an article in *USA Today*, multiple experts agreed that heavy workloads for students have the potential for more harm than good. Emmy Kang, a mental health counselor at Humantold, shared that "more than half of students say that homework is their primary source of stress," adding that working long hours to complete assignments can lead to exhaustion. Similarly, Cynthia Catchings, a licensed clinical social worker and therapist at Talkspace, reported that students who are assigned a lot of homework can develop problems like anxiety and depression. And Dr. Nicholas Kardaras, a psychologist and the CEO of Omega Recovery, suggested that schoolwork should not go home at all, saying that the research demonstrates that "there's really limited benefit of homework for elementary age students."*

While there's a lot of research that supports Dr. Kardaras's conclusion about not assigning homework for younger kids, there's still a pretty entrenched belief that older students need it. The belief is that kids won't thrive in college without the habit of completing academic work—whether that's reading or doing math problems—on their own. But a recent NEA article pointed out one teacher who's proving those beliefs wrong in Wisconsin. When Scott Anderson started teaching math in 2006, he used to assign thirty math problems to his students on an almost daily basis.

When test scores came back, he realized that his students weren't learning. To make things worse, he realized there was a gap between students who had access to help and the Internet at home and those who didn't. Given that homework accounted for 25 percent of a student's grade, the inequity among his students influenced their report cards, which could potentially make or break college admissions. Mr. Anderson did the research on homework and decided to decrease the amount of homework he gave each night.

Mr. Anderson made three key changes in his classroom as a result. First, he reduced the number of homework math problems from thirty to twelve. Second, instead of lecturing for the majority of class, he decided to spend only ten minutes

*Sarah M. Moniuszko, "Is It Time to Get Rid of Homework? Mental Health Experts Weigh In," *USA Today*, August 16, 2021, https://www.usatoday.com/story/life/health-wellness/2021/08/16/students -mental-health-time-get-rid-homework-schools/5536050001.

teaching and the rest of the time working on math problems in person with his students. And lastly, he changed how grades were calculated. Mr. Anderson lowered how much homework counted toward a student's grade significantly, to 1 percent, and put more weight on quizzes and tests that students could retake until they mastered the material.

At first, parents grumbled because the amount of As in his class decreased by one-fifth. But then something remarkable happened. The students in Scott's school went from 30 percent ready for college math to nearly 100 percent ready.

"Our job in high school is to guarantee that students pick up these skills. That's my mandate, which is different from a college professor's, in my opinion," said Mr. Anderson. "I believe strongly that my students are much better at math now than they were a decade ago."*

Homework isn't fair.

The reality is that everyone does not have access to the same tools, support, and time to complete work outside of the classroom. Some students have a computer and high-speed Internet service. They have a bookshelf filled with their favorite books. Some students have a parent who sits at the table and assists with all their homework assignments. They check all of the work and quiz their child on the spelling words each day. This is not the case for every student in your class.

Some students are latch-key kids. Maybe they help care for siblings after school. Some students do not have Internet access at all, or perhaps they have slow Internet service and one device that they share with the entire family. You may have students who do not have access to engaging books at home. And I am certain that you

---

*Tim Walker, "A High School Teacher Scrapped Homework. Here's What Happened Next," *NEA Today*, November 15, 2019, https://www.nea.org/advocating-for-change/new-from-nea/high-school -teacher-scrapped-homework-heres-what-happened-next.

have students who do not have a parent who has the time to be able to sit down and help with each homework assignment. Maybe they are working two jobs, or they might be a single parent balancing work and multiple children. Either way, every student in your class does not have equal access to support and tools to complete their homework.

When you assign homework and then grade it, you are often assessing parent support rather than what a student knows.

Homework doesn't help kids to grow academically.

Typically we teach a lesson and then send home an assignment based on the lesson we just taught. We are assigning homework based on a brand-new skill rather than one we have worked on in small groups and centers. For this reason, our highest learners do well with the homework and our lowest learners continue to struggle. So the kids who already know it will do fine and the kids who haven't learned it yet will struggle. That is not growth.

Students grow when they receive differentiated support and participate in engaging lessons that increase their love for learning—not by completing a worksheet.

Without the support, anchor charts, manipulatives, and other tools that you provide in the classroom, most students are likely to perform at a lower level. This can lead to frustration and even bad habits that are hard to break later.

Homework teaches the habit of overworking.

I am hoping to help break you of the habit of working a full day and then bringing home more work. Unfortunately, it's a habit that was born at the age of five or six. By kindergarten or first grade, children are going to school for about eight hours and then bringing more work home. After a full day of learning, which is so incredibly exhausting, children are not free. They still have more work. We are literally teaching them that working for eight hours per day is not enough. This is a lesson that will not serve them well as adults in the workforce. This is how we end up with adults who are burned out and lack self-care skills.

Instead, children should be able to come home from school and ride bikes, play board games, and try new hobbies. They need time to learn a musical instrument or a sport. More than anything, they need time to rest and be with family and friends.

When the bell rings, let work be done for the day.

There are other ways to teach responsibility.

Children learn responsibility by helping to take care of their classroom, checking out library books, learning how to properly use playground equipment, and keeping their desk and folders organized. They also learn responsibility at home by helping to care for siblings and pets, doing household chores, and earning an allowance. The great thing about all these responsibility lessons is that they have true real-world applications. The children are learning practical skills that they will need as an adult. Homework is not the only way to teach responsibility.

If you can at all get away with it, do not assign homework to your students. It will be so freeing! You will save loads of time prepping and grading papers. It may surprise some families, but with some explanation, they will come around. If they truly want homework, suggest that they spend more time reading with their child and perhaps create a journal where they can write letters back and forth with one another. These are healthy ways to practice what they are learning at school without the pressure of nightly graded assignments.

Now, I get it. Sometimes your hands are tied because your administration requires teachers to assign homework. I've been there. If you have to send home assignments, commit to the following:

- Send home as little as possible. Ten minutes per night of homework is plenty!
- Send home assignments that are a true review of skills you have taught in class. Give students time to practice and master these skills before sending home an independent assignment. This will help more of your students be successful with the tools and support available to them at home.
- Don't grade the homework. You can choose one problem and quickly scan to see how well students did with that particular problem. This can help inform future whole-group or small-group lessons. You can give completion points. Whatever you do, don't spend hours grading every single problem. After all, you don't know if the problems were completed by the student or the parent.

Strategy #4 • DON'T GRADE TOO MANY CENTERS.

I used to take a grade on every darn center my students completed during a week. I did this for reading and math. It was nuts, but I thought it was the only way to hold my students accountable. If I didn't give everything a grade, why would they bother completing the assignment? Over time, I learned the answer. My elementary students rarely completed an assignment in order to get a certain grade. Honestly, grades weren't a huge motivation for the majority of my students. They completed assignments when they understood the expectations and felt confident with the skills being tested. Basically, most of my students would complete their center work if they felt like they could be successful. We are always more likely to do the things we feel good at. When this became apparent to me, I started to include more review work in centers and I stopped grading every single center.

I am not saying you shouldn't take a grade for centers at all. Taking a grade on some centers is a great way to meet those pesky minimum-grade requirements. Centers are also a great way for students to show what they know—especially if the centers review skills they have had lots of time to master. Just don't get carried away. I had four different rotations during centers. (As you know, we did only two rotations per day. You can read more about that in chapter 4.) I took a grade from only one of those four rotations and it wasn't even weekly.

In reading, I took a grade on the reading-response activity. However, since this is a short writing piece, it can take more time to grade. Therefore, I would grade half the class's pieces one week and the other half's the next week. (And no, my students did not know I was doing this. It did not decrease their motivation.) All my students received a grade on this center every other week. This cut my grading time in half on that one center.

For math centers, I took a grade on our individual hands-on center. This center was a set of ten different activities that my students would complete over a month. Therefore, I had to grade their booklets only once per month.

Another option is to have students grade their own centers. You can give them answer keys and model how you want them to be scored. Start by practicing this routine together as a class. Gradually release control and allow your students to check their own work. Will there be mistakes in their scoring? Absolutely. But is that the hill that you want to die on? Are you willing to accept a few errors in order to remove some grading from your weekly schedule? If so, it's worth a try! After all, what is the best that could happen?

Looking for opportunities to take fewer grades from your centers is a great way to save time. Some easy options are:

- Decrease the number of center activities you grade.
- Don't feel obligated to grade centers every week.
- Teach students to self-grade.
- Spot-check center activities during small groups to make sure students are on track.

Strategy #5 • MAKE YOUR ASSESSMENTS EASIER TO GRADE.

If we have to grade, and we do, the least we can do for ourselves is make the assignment easy to grade. Here are a few ways I simplified and sped up my grading.

Look for multiple-choice.

Administrators may not necessarily agree with me on this one, but as you have probably noticed, I like to push the boundaries. There is no reason that every assessment should be a short answer or an essay. Certainly there is a time and a place for higher-order-thinking assessments, but it does not have to be the norm. It's perfectly okay to have multiple-choice or true/false assessments. They are quick to administer and super quick to grade. At the same time, they are a simple way to check for understanding. Look for these types of quick assessments whenever possible.

Don't forget about self-grading assessments.

Pandemic teaching was a little like flying an airplane without a pilot's license while on fire. It was truly a hot mess. But one of the great things to come out of a pretty crappy time is that teachers and students became more aware and confident about using technology. Schools even started to invest more money into computers, Chromebooks, and iPads. There are amazing apps and software programs that make it easy to assign a quiz and have the program grade it for you. One of the most common is Google Forms. There is nothing more satisfying than logging into your Google Classroom and seeing that your grades are already tabulated. Don't forget about these amazing tools.

Strategy #6 • SPEED UP THE GRADING OF WRITTEN RESPONSES.

Multiple-choice assessments are my very best friends, but I understand the value and the need to grade written responses, reports, and essays. These types of assessments show deeper thinking and are part of our standards. They won't be the bulk of my grades, but they will appear on that report card from time to time. This type of grading most certainly takes longer, but there are a few ways to save some time.

Use a simple rubric.

Having a simple rubric makes it so much easier to assign grades on written responses and remain consistent. The rubric also helps students and parents understand the expectations for writing assignments. The key is to make sure that the rubric is super simple. If it is very wordy or confusing, it will just slow you down. I also love to have my students complete their essays on paper with a small copy of the rubric photocopied on the bottom. Now you don't have to waste time stapling rubrics to essays.

Don't mark up their errors.

There is nothing more discouraging as a writer than having every single spelling and grammar mistake circled in red ink for you. I know. When I create resources for teachers, I want them to be the highest quality possible. After I create a resource, a teammate or two will edit it for me. Once I think it's in pretty good shape, I send it to a professional editor just to be on the safe side. Every time she sends it back with red lines under almost every darn word. I'm always shocked by how many mistakes I can make. You would think I was typing in the dark or maybe that I had my three-year-old create the resource. Perhaps my college French professor was right and I don't know English at all. It's pretty disheartening.

It feels even worse for your students. They put so much effort into their writing. It is their masterpiece. They think you will be impressed. When you mark up every error, they are deflated. It decreases their confidence and their love for writing.

And do they become better writers because you pointed out every error? Absolutely not! There is no way they will learn how to properly spell every word you circled. They will not suddenly start to implement every grammar rule because of the ink marks on this paper. All those skills just take tons of time and practice. The truth is that you are only improving that particular piece of writing rather than helping the writer grow. A better practice is to choose one or two words that they used often or will potentially be able to use on other writing samples. Show them how to spell just those words and leave the other errors unmarked. You can take off points on the rubric for spelling without circling every misspelled word.

Marking up every error takes a ton of time too. When you ditch this practice, you will be able to grade your written responses in a fraction of the time. Doesn't that sound amazing?

Don't write comments.

We love to write notes as we grade.

"Great lead! I am hooked."

"I also love to get cotton candy at the fair!"

"I'd love to see you expand this paragraph and share more details about what dolphins eat."

We are just trying to help. And to be real honest, I think we are trying to prove or justify the grade we are giving on the rubric. But writing comment after comment just adds to the ink on the page. Many of your comments won't be read (I actually found that my students couldn't read my writing!). Even more important, the practice of writing comments really slows down your grading. It's a time sucker.

Let the rubric be your communication with your students. Teach them how to read the rubric. If they received full credit for their lead, they know that you liked their lead without you having to write a note. And you can always talk to them about your shared love for cotton candy at recess or during a break. It will go a long way in building that student relationship!

Strategy #7 • ASK FOR HELP.

I love to ask parent volunteers to help with the simple grading! I often had a couple parents or grandparents who would volunteer for a few hours per week. They could easily grade spelling tests, math-fact tests, and any other multiple choice assessments. Depending on the volunteer, I could often give them a key and have them grade the math-center booklets. Parent volunteers can also check off homework for completion if that is something you have to assign. I would have them record the scores on a spreadsheet, and this made it easy for me to review the scores and add them to the gradebook.

Now, I know every school doesn't allow parent volunteers. Even if your school does allow parent volunteers, they may not allow them to do student grading. (At my school, the volunteers had to sign a confidentiality agreement stating that they could not share any grades outside of the classroom.) Just make me a deal: Do not write this one off until you have asked! Do not just assume your admin will say no. Do not just assume your classroom parents will not want to help. You might be very surprised! It's worth a shot.

Strategy #8 • STOP GRADING IN FRONT OF THE TV.

I might lose some friends over this one, but know that I am only saying this because I want the best for you. I want you to have the strategies to meet your definition of success, and for most of you that means working less.

Often, teachers in the Not So Wimpy Teacher community will talk about how they like to grade in front of the TV because it makes the time go by faster. I totally agree. Time flies by when I park it on the couch and binge-watch HGTV.

I also know this is true: I sit down to grade in front of my favorite TV shows. Hours later I am shocked by how late it is and how the night got away from me. I enjoyed watching my show, but I look down and notice that I have barely touched the pile of papers that I had planned to grade.

Watching TV is fun.

Watching TV makes time go faster.

And watching TV kills your productivity.

Instead, spend some time completing your grading and then enjoy your shows guilt-free!

Where's the Craziest Place You've Graded?

I polled our Not So Wimpy Facebook communities and got some amazing answers. If you've been there and done that, you're not alone!

"I graded in a casino/hotel bar. We were killing time before my husband's Christmas party, watching basketball games. I sat at the bar top with my markers and stack of papers to grade."　**—Alexa K.**

"Sitting in the OB doctor's office waiting for test results. I couldn't leave so I brought my file crate and rolling computer bag with all of my pretty pens and grade book. Three people came and went . . . observing and commenting 'you're a teacher, aren't you?'"

—Sharon

"My husband and his best friend were brewery-hopping for a friend's birthday. I didn't want them to drive after drinking, so I worked on grading stuff while sitting at the breweries . . . on my day off."

—Christina

"At a bachelorette party!"

—Andrea

"Church. Faithfully. I was the only person sitting in the balcony and I always had my laptop, work to be graded, and my colorful pens and still managed to listen to the sermon and shout an 'Amen, Pastor!' when I was supposed to. My church started at 11 and didn't get out until 1:30. I made sure I used my time wisely 💋"

—Kay Renee

"On a pontoon boat going down the Indian River in Edgewater, Florida!"

—Marilyn Marie

Strategy #9 • PUT GRADING ON THE CALENDAR.

I'm going to repeat myself here. After all, I am a teacher and repeating ourselves is one of our many talents. We already spent an entire chapter talking about how to plan your nonteaching time using your calendar. But there is no way that I could complete this chapter on grading and not remind you of the importance of putting your grading time on the calendar. So consider this your review lesson.

If it doesn't go on the calendar, it doesn't get done.

The only way to make sure something gets completed is to set aside and prioritize the time to make it happen. As you plan for your week (check out chapter 2 for more tips on this), make sure you are deciding on the exact times you will use for grading. It is not just a to-do list, but an actual time that is blocked out, like a meeting with your grading. Some people like to put a little time every day on their calendar for grading. Others prefer to block out a large chunk of time one or two days per week for their grading. You may have to experiment to decide which method works best for you.

Once you have marked off time on your calendar to complete your weekly grading, I want you to take it one step further. Decide exactly what you will finish grading during that time. This is different from a list of things you should grade or will work on grading. I want you to be very specific and realistic as you decide exactly what you will finish during your grading time. Maybe you have time to grade only five opinion-writing essays or ten of the unit-six math tests. Whatever it is, declare it on your calendar. When it comes time to grade, you will have a very clear plan for success. At the end of your scheduled time, you won't feel guilty about the stack of papers you didn't grade. Instead, you can feel proud of the papers you planned to grade and finished grading.

Strategy #10 • MAKE IT AS FUN AS POSSIBLE.

When done properly, grading is as fun as drinking fruity beverages on the beach while the Backstreet Boys serenade you with your favorite nineties tunes.

Bazinga!

Grading isn't fun and I refuse to lie to you and tell you otherwise. I wish I could make it a blast for you, but I am not a magician or a genie. Even though grading is not likely to be your favorite part of the job, there are some things that can make it a little less miserable. The best way to make grading less of a chore is to spend less of your time grading. That has been the main focus of this chapter and I hope you found two or three strategies that will cut back your grading time.

If you are looking for some more ways to add a hint of fun, try some of these ideas:

Choose your pen wisely.

Go to your local office supply store and stock up on your favorite pens. (I prefer the scented Paper Mate Flair pens. They smell amazing!) Grading with your favorite pen can make the chore slightly more enjoyable.

Don't forget the refreshments.

Are you sitting down for a long time block of grading? Make it more fun by treating yourself to your favorite snack and beverage. You need the extra energy, right?

Give yourself a trip to the prize box.

Okay, maybe you don't want to sift through your student prize box for a smelly sticker or a glow-in-the-dark ring. Instead, decide on a simple reward to gift yourself when the grading is complete. This might be having dinner delivered instead of cooking, or maybe it's a thirty-minute walk with your dog. Working toward a reward makes everything more fun.

Now that you've got these ten strategies, are you committed to spending less time grading? I am not trying to be over-the-top and dramatic, but I honestly believe that these strategies made a huge impact on my marriage and family life.

When I was teaching in the classroom, my husband was a nurse at a pediatric hospital. He worked the night shift, which meant that he started at 7:00 p.m. and got off at 7:00 a.m. His sleep schedule was very erratic due to days off and the fact that we had four kids.

Almost every Friday, I would send him a text that looked something like this: "Would you be willing to just take a short nap and then come to my classroom to help grade? I have so many papers to grade and I'm stressed. Oh! And bring a Coke, please!"

He almost always came. He would grade homework packets and spelling tests while nearly falling asleep at my volunteer table. Sometimes I actually had to nudge him awake. I'm ashamed to admit that I prioritized grading papers over my husband's health and sleep needs. He loved me enough to say "yes," but I love him enough to say "no more."

If you have time to do only one thing
from this chapter, I want you to:

Stop grading homework.

Homework is not fair, doesn't teach responsibility, and can encourage kids

to overwork as adults. If at all possible, I give you full permission to stop

giving homework altogether!

The Not So Wimpy Way to Grade

1. Stop grading everything (pages 127–128).

2. Use more informal assessments (pages 129–130).

3. Don't grade (or give) homework (pages 131–136).

4. Don't grade too many centers (pages 136–138).

5. Make your assessments easier to grade (pages 138–139).

6. Speed up the grading of written responses (pages 139–141).

7. Stop grading in front of the TV (pages 142–144).

8. Put grading on the calendar (page 145).

Optional:

- Ask for help (page 142).

- Make grading fun (pages 146–147).

CHAPTER SIX

Keep Your Eyes on Your Own Paper

hen I had my first baby, I remember being so shocked that the nurses and doctors were just going to let me take him home from the hospital. Isn't there a test I should have to take to prove I am capable of keeping a tiny human alive? What if someone finds out I have never changed a diaper or burped a baby?

I felt the exact same way on my first day of teaching. That day was literally the first time I had ever been alone in a room with twenty-five third graders. I was petrified. Shouldn't there be someone in here making sure I don't screw up? What the heck am I supposed to say to them? Can they smell my fear?

I realized that I needed to learn a whole heck of a lot more to become an effective teacher for my class. Lucky for me, there was another third-grade teacher right across the hall.

Sheri taught me how to be a teacher. (Because, let's be honest, the college courses did not prepare me for the classroom.) I would get to school early every morning and, without an invitation, plant myself in Sheri's classroom. While she was preparing for her day, I would pepper her with all my questions. Some were super silly and others were incredibly vulnerable.

Where do I get copy paper?

Is there a pencil sharpener that won't break after a week?

What should I do if I have a student who doesn't know any of her sight words?

How do you fit everything into the day?

Is my dress too short?

Was it a mistake for me to teach third grade without any experience?

Sheri was incredibly patient and generous with me. Not only did she answer all of my questions (even the super-personal ones), but she shared resources and even had some of her parent volunteers help my class. She always smiled and told me that I was doing great.

One Friday morning, I was in Sheri's room before school and she was putting sheet music on her students' desks. "Wait, you teach music too?!" She explained that on Fridays she liked to do a music appreciation lesson. I lost it. I could barely manage to teach reading, writing, and math. Sheri was teaching all of that *and* music appreciation! How was that even possible?

Later that day I sat in the principal's office crying big ugly tears.

(I mean—are you even a teacher if you haven't sat in the principal's office crying?)

I tried to tell my principal how terrible I was as a teacher. I just couldn't do it like Sheri. The principal looked me right in the eyes and said, "Stop trying to be like

Sheri! No one can be like her." I totally didn't understand. Why wouldn't I want to be like Sheri? She appeared to be the perfect teacher. Students, parents, and co-workers seemed to love her. That is exactly what I wanted.

I wish I could tell you that I listened to my very wise principal on that day.

But at the time, I didn't understand. I wanted to be the perfect teacher . . . and there she was, right across the hall from me teaching freaking music appreciation. At the time, I thought my principal was telling me not to compare myself to Sheri. But that was only one part of her advice. What she actually wanted me to do was to give up trying to be like Sheri—*and*, instead, focus on finding the best way to be me, Mrs. Sears.

Eventually, I did learn how I could be an effective teacher. I figured out what worked for me and what didn't. And a lot of those strategies are in this book. Some may work for you and others may not. As teachers, I think there's an idea that we're being graded too.

Social media makes it easy to compare ourselves to other teachers. We scroll through Pinterest and Instagram and we see perfectly decorated and organized classrooms. We read about elaborate classroom activities that cost a fortune and take a month to plan.

Those Pinterest-perfect teachers obviously get straight As, and us . . . well, maybe we figure out how to get a B on a good day. It's no wonder teachers feel like they are failing. I know that I did. In my first year teaching, I pretty much assumed I was getting a big fat F . . . that did not stand for fun.

Looking back, part of that was because, despite getting really good advice from my principal, I continued to observe Sheri's every move. I did my best to implement almost everything I saw in her classroom. (Luckily for everyone, I skipped the music appreciation class.) I was killing myself comparing my teaching and my classroom to Sheri every day.

And after I discovered social media and Pinterest . . . my comparison habit got worse.

Teachers from all over the country were sharing all their amazing ideas. From classroom decor to holiday parties to elaborate anchor charts—I had thousands of new teacher mentors. It was like having thousands of Sheris, right there on my phone. I continued to model everything I learned from Sheri and then just added more with every new pin or Instagram post I saw. I felt like literally every teacher out there was more creative, more innovative, and more effective than me. Keeping up with these amazing teachers was exhausting and defeating. I just couldn't compare. It's so easy to assume that what everyone else is doing in their classroom works like a charm and is executed flawlessly . . . when in reality every single teacher is learning what works and what doesn't on a daily basis. That's why it's best to keep your eyes on your own paper and figure out how to set your own curve instead of striving for someone else's perfect grade.

If you've ever found yourself racing to keep up with other teachers at your school or failing to implement the strategies "perfect" teachers share online, this chapter is for you.

GREAT TEACHERS LET GO OF "PERFECT."

I was an avid scrapbooker when my teenagers were young. My husband's closet shelves are filled with the dozens of overflowing albums I created for the kids. (They can't go in my closet because that is where my shoe collection lives.) I even went to scrapbooking clubs and parties. The highlight of every year back then was the scrapbook convention. That's where hundreds of vendors sell the latest and greatest in scrapbook paper, tools, and embellishments. I bought way too much, but I had so much fun that it didn't matter.

And even though I loved collecting all the pretty things, I knew that scrapbooking is all about the stories, not the stickers. The pages tell the stories of my kids' childhood. In those scrapbooks I share what it was like to experience their births, their first words, their typical days as second graders, and the funny things they said along the way. The stories are told through the pictures and the journaling I thoughtfully added to every page—not the embellishments I added to the story. The items I bought at the scrapbooking conventions make the page cute, but they aren't necessary. The story is the only mandatory element of a scrapbook page. The story has the leading role in the scrapbook. Everything else is just an extra.

Similarly, in the world of theater the actors play the leading roles. The majority of practice time is spent running their lines, digging into their characters' personality traits, and choreographing their movement. The set and the props are not added until the very end. The reality is that you can have a show without sets and props. Those are the extras. A show without sets or props may not be as visually appealing, but it is still possible. But there can't be a show without the actors.

In your classroom, students have the leading role. Your relationship with the students in your classroom is the most important thing. What you see on social media or in the classroom across the hall are generally the bells and whistles, the extras. These aspects of your classroom and teaching aren't essential and therefore shouldn't be the first thing you add.

After you have created a student-centered classroom, you can start to think about things like classroom themes, room transformations, morning meetings, passion projects, or whatever activity is currently trending on social media. These activities can add a lot to your classroom, just like stickers add to a scrapbook page and props add to a theatrical production. But in all these scenarios—especially teaching— a little can go a long way. Focus on the leading role and then add the extras later.

Jerriline, a teacher in the Not So Wimpy community, put it this way: "It takes quite a few years to realize that you will never know enough, do enough, or be enough." In her second year of teaching, she realized that trying to be the "perfect teacher" will make you desperately unhappy. There was a teacher in her school whose students outperformed all the other classes, who practically lived at the school, and who was always jumping on board every time the district had some new program.

This teacher was constantly stressed-out and cranky. No matter the results she was getting in her classroom, Jerriline didn't want to be her.

The lesson is simple: teachers only need to love learning, love kids, and love their lives. This is the hallmark of a truly great teacher.

ere are my favorite two strategies to stay focused on what's happening in your classroom. (This is where I use all my theater references. See, Mom, I told you those college courses would come in handy!)

DON'T COMPARE YOUR BACKSTAGE TO THEIR FRONT STAGE.

I was in *The Nutcracker* ballet four years in a row when I was in high school. Don't let that fool you into thinking that I was a talented dancer. The choreographer once walked by me and said, "Wow, your arms are terrible." I didn't have years and years of dance classes as a child like some of the other members of the cast. I didn't even really like dancing. I just liked being onstage. My practices were grueling. I had to stay late to run my part a few more times . . . most nights. On top of that, I had to schedule extra private rehearsals. My muscles hurt. I received some hard-to-hear criticism and sometimes there were tears. But by the time performance came, I was able to perform the dance without error. I fit right in with the rest of the cast. What the audience saw was polished. They saw the front stage that night. They never saw the pain and tears backstage as I prepared for those eight glorious moments of *Nutcracker* fame.

When we see those amazing teachers across the hall or online, we see only their front stage. We see the polished version rather than the first attempt. We see the edited photo, but not the mess behind the camera. We very rarely get to see the work, frustration, and doubt from backstage. Because we can't see it, we start to assume that the front stage is the whole story.

Let me be very clear: everyone has a backstage—even the most popular and polished teachers on social media. You might see your mentor teacher do the most engaging lesson. What you don't see is the hours of time she spent over the weekend preparing the materials. You might see the most beautiful classroom on Insta-gram. What you don't see is the credit-card bill

"I'm in my first year of teaching. I have an amazing team who helps me with any question I may have. Getting to know them and seeing some of the things they do does make me feel like I should be doing more than I am.

But I tell myself that I am a first year teacher and they are veteran teachers. Next year will be way better since I know how the year goes. Next year I know what to expect and I can do a little more. I do feel like sometimes I'm not reaching my kids and that I should be doing more. But when I talk to my kids and see how they are progressing, they are doing wonderful."

—Jessica J.

and the stress caused by overspending. You might see the most creative reading room transformation on Pinterest. What you don't see is the doubt and lack of confidence that the same teacher has when teaching math each day. I saw Sheri teaching music theory. What I didn't see was her staying up until the early morning hours sending emails and putting together her lesson plans. Even Sheri had a backstage. All of our backstages look different, but we all have one.

DON'T COMPARE YOUR FIRST ACT TO THEIR SECOND ACT.

Nearly every day I receive an email from a teacher asking me how to make money selling teacher resources online. Most of them don't want the truth. They want me to give them some super-amazing secret that will allow them to make tons of money right away. They want to skip straight to financial success. The truth is that it takes years of creating content and serving your teacher audience while creating and then re-creating your resources until they are good enough to meet the needs of other teachers. (If you're interested in learning more, you can find resources for how to start your own business at notsowimpyteacher.com/bookresources.)

It's taken me a decade to get my business to the place it is now. With a great mentor, I am certain someone could get to this place quicker than I did, but it will not happen overnight. You can't compare your new store to my established store.

That was exactly what I was doing with Sheri. She had been teaching for decades. Then little ol' me walked in and thought I could teach just like her without putting in all the time she had put in. I convinced myself I could just skip all those lessons, the hard work, and even the tears.

It's fine to have a teacher you admire the way I admired Sheri. In fact, if you haven't already, I highly recommend that you find a mentor you can learn from. The problem comes when we think we need to be just like our mentor today rather than eventually implementing some of their strategies. Give yourself time. Don't attempt to skip all the scenes that come between the first act and the second act.

Okay—so if it's not what we see on Pinterest or in the classroom next door that makes for effective teaching, what does? Back when I was teaching at the school with Sheri, I was really struggling. Even if I had listened to my principal and had stopped trying to imitate Sheri, I still would have been teaching my lessons to the whole group. As most of you probably know already, that method of teaching makes it nearly impossible to differentiate. I would also still be struggling to engage my students in the lessons, basically talking to myself all day. And I would still be trying to make every day and every lesson different rather than creating routines my students could depend on.

My point is that even without Sheri, I would have still been a scared teacher with ineffective lessons. I had to do something different! I think first-year teacher-me knew that and was trying to find the answer by watching Sheri.

It can be tough to be more effective in the classroom without doing too much or opening Pinterest. But here are two tried-by-me strategies that worked, no app needed.

TRY ONE NEW THING AT A TIME.

So many of us struggle to figure out how to find new, simple, and effective strategies to improve what we do day in, day out in our classrooms. Obviously, I couldn't do everything Sheri was doing—and I was burning myself out trying everything new I saw online. But the problem wasn't the new ideas or the inspiration Sheri was providing nearly every day.

Instead, it was how I chose to implement what inspired me. Sometimes, we need to try something new to land on something great. But that can be hard. For example, I am not proud of this, but I *still* eat like a two-year-old. It's an embarrassing confession to make, but my favorite foods are Kraft macaroni and cheese, fried chicken tenders, and McDonald's cheeseburgers.

I don't eat vegetables. You can't even trick me by hiding them in my mac and cheese.

In 2019, I had the honor of getting to speak on my mentor's stage. Amy Porterfield is someone I love to learn from, and she helped me create an online course that makes teaching writing easier for educators across the country. When she asked me to join her onstage in front of a thousand people, I was starstruck.

Before the presentation, she invited me to have lunch with her. I was excited but crazy nervous. I didn't want my idol to find out that I eat like a toddler. When I approached the table for lunch, all my worst fears came true. A salad was at my spot. I would tell you what veggies were on the salad, but I honestly have no clue. Everything on that plate was foreign to me. It looked like rabbit food. But the salad was the least of my concerns. When the main dish was served, my heart sank into my stomach. On top of even more vegetables was grilled salmon.

I *never* eat fish. The closest thing I would put near my mouth before that moment was Goldfish crackers. But I really didn't want to look like a fool in front of Amy. So I did the big-girl thing and ate the dang fish. Not all of it, but enough that no one noticed. Under the table I sent a text to my husband that said, "Oh my gosh. I am eating fish."

I know I said that sometimes we need to try something new to find something great, like, a page ago. But I want to be clear—I didn't go home and start cooking fish every night for dinner. In fact, I really didn't care for the fish and I haven't eaten another bite since that day. I may not have discovered a hidden love for seafood, but I am proud that I tried it. I proved to myself that I am the kind of person who can try new things.

Trying new things is so dang scary.

But—trying new things is also a key to loving teaching again.

"But, Jamie, who has time to try new things? I thought you wanted us to do less, not more."

Let me explain.

When I was a brand-spankin'-new teacher in that school with Sheri, everything was new to me. I ran reading groups for the first time. I introduced my first classroom-management system. I threw my very first classroom parties and cele-brations. I had so many ideas and most of the time my excitement could not be contained. (Not doing a music appreciation lesson might be one of the exceptions.) I was finally doing what I had spent four years of college just talking about.

But there was a problem—and I bet you've had it too. I was crazy excited and determined to do everything I saw other teachers doing, but because everything was new, I grew tired very quickly. I had trouble keeping up. There were too many new things to learn and prepare for. Even my laminator couldn't keep up; it died that school year.

But here's the thing: What if you commit to trying *just* one new thing in your classroom?

Doing the same thing over and over again can get so boring. Getting out of a rut and experimenting can bring so much energy and excitement back to teaching. But limiting yourself to just one new thing will help you avoid comparison overwhelm (and prolong the life of your laminator). There's no need to do everything you've ever pinned to your school Pinterest board all at once. All that leads to is half-baked bulletin boards and a pile of lamination by your bed. Trust me, I know.

If I can eat fish, you can do this.

Let's start by picking your first *new* project. (Yay!)

Here are some tips to help you to prioritize and choose that one new thing.

Most importantly, I want you to choose something that *you* want to do. Not whatever your teacher bestie is doing, or what's popular on Instagram right now, or what your principal thinks everyone should do. Ask yourself: What excites *you*? If you're looking at the Pinterest board, what's the image that makes you feel dreamy and happy? Your new project needs to be something that feels right to you and brings you joy.

Next, let's consider time. (Most people skip this process and jump into everything that excites them. But you aren't like most people. You are so intentional with your time now.)

How much time do these new project ideas require?

Will you need to take professional development or read a book?

Will you need to prep materials?

Is this a project you will slowly implement throughout the year, or is this a project that will be complete within a couple of weeks?

After you have considered the time requirements for the projects you have on your wish list, take a look at your calendar. How much time can you honestly devote to trying something new? We want to pick only projects we can fit into our work hours. Some of your ideas might be great, but they aren't right for you now in your season of life and teaching. It's okay to recognize that a project needs to be put on hold for now. It doesn't mean that you'll never get to take on that new idea. It just means that you are currently saying "not yet" because you are saying "yes" to other things.

Finally, consider the impact of the project you are considering.

Which project on your list will have the greatest return on your effort?

Is there a project on your wish list that will decrease your stress during the year?

Is there a project that will lead to higher student performance?

For example, if you hate teaching writing and it causes you stress every day, then taking a course and implementing a new writing workshop can decrease that daily stress. If classroom management brings you to tears, then starting a new management program could be the answer to happier days. You might want to choose the project that will give you the biggest impact, but it's perfectly fine to choose the project that is easiest right now. Every season is different and you get to decide what feels good now.

Are you struggling to think of a good new project?

Here are some ideas, but remember that they are just ideas. This is *not* a list of things you "should" be doing in your classroom.

- Take a professional development course on your least favorite subject to teach.
- Redo your center rotations to be easier to manage. (Or start using centers if you haven't already.)
- Research and implement a new classroom-management program.
- Start book clubs with your reading groups.
- Implement STEM or STEAM activities in your classroom.

Finding one new thing to learn, change, or implement in your classroom can bring so much life back to teaching. Keeping your eyes on your own paper (aka classroom), and not feeling like you need to keep up with the teacher down the hall, is liberating! Give yourself permission to focus on one new thing at a time, because we want your teaching career to be a marathon rather than a sprint. Sprinting, or making a million changes all at once, is just not sustainable.

Learning how to tackle something new is actually crucial for teachers. Our career is an endless stream of new things and evolving demands. It can feel like we're given a new curriculum practically every day. Or that we're asked every single year to teach a different grade level or adapt to new standards. As much fun as it is to choose our own project to implement in the classroom, the reality is that we are going to be required to make changes that are mandated by our district or our supervisor. There is no way around it. This is just part of the teaching career.

EXPECT CHANGE.

I had been teaching for only two years when I found myself buried deep in new curriculum. We were given a new math curriculum (for the second year in a row) and a new writing curriculum during the same year. Of course, we were mandated to use them exclusively and we were not given any training on either program. I spent hours and hours trying to read the dozens of teacher guides that come with these new curriculums. Sound familiar? My confidence while teaching math and writing was at an all-time low during this particular year. And to be real honest, my love for teaching was at a dangerously low point as well. It was all very overwhelming.

I wish I could tell you that I have this super-secret strategy for eliminating radical and unnecessary change that is mandated by someone else. I'd be every teacher's very best friend if I could get my hands on that strategy. Y'all would be fighting over who got to sit next to me at the next staff meeting. This is the part where I give you the bad news. There is no such strategy. Change is inevitable. You will get new curriculum. Your admin will come up with a new pet project. You will get a new schedule. You will probably even have to change grade levels at some point.

You can choose to feel overwhelmed by the change or you can choose to strategically make a plan that helps you implement the change with the least amount of distress possible. Choose option two! You may not be able to eliminate change, but you can decide how to handle the change.

I have pulled together some of my favorite tips (and a few from my teacher community) for handling a new curriculum, a new school, and a new grade level. Use these tips to help create a plan that makes you feel like you have some control and empowerment in the face of new demands.

New Curriculum

- Intentionally set aside time for reviewing and learning how to use the curriculum before you have to start using it in the classroom. Get out your calendar and choose time blocks for researching, brainstorming, preparing, and planning. Start by researching and learning about the curriculum and what is required. Then take some time to brainstorm how the components of the curriculum can be used and fit into your classroom routine. Prepare any printables. Finally, integrate the new curriculum into your lesson plans.

- Focus on one small part of the curriculum at a time. Most programs come with tons of pieces. Don't try to incorporate every piece on day one. Learn just one component at a time and slowly add the pieces into your classroom a little at a time. Instead of jumping right in and drowning, wade in slowly. This will increase your confidence and decrease your overwhelm.

- Check the curriculum website for resources that they have created. Often, these companies have created training videos all about implementing their curriculum. Understanding the why behind each of the components in the program can make a huge difference when deciding how to roll it out in your classroom. Depending on funds, you might encourage your administration to bring a trainer to your school or district. Getting to ask questions is life changing!
- Look for Facebook groups that include other teachers who use the curriculum so that you have a place to ask questions and get support. Other teachers have been where you are now. Someone who is further into the journey can be a wealth of tips when it comes to actually using the curriculum in the classroom. You can easily search for curriculum-specific groups on Facebook.

Moving to a New School or Grade Level

- Look for a mentor right away. Whether you are at a new school or teaching a new grade, you are going to need someone to go to with your questions. Usually your next-door-neighbor teacher or the team lead are great options for a mentor. Be certain that you are respecting their time. Most teachers are happy to help a new teammate, but you don't want to assume they can drop everything whenever you walk into their room. Try to schedule time with them, or send some questions via email so that they can answer when it is convenient for them.
- Get familiar with the curriculum as soon as possible. If you are faced with new curriculum (or standards) in multiple subjects, consider tackling one

subject at a time. Use the tips from above to help immerse yourself in the new programs without getting terribly overwhelmed.

- Intentionally spend more time listening than talking. When we are working with a new team, there is a tendency to want to prove ourselves to them. We go in with all of our ideas and ways that things should be done in the classroom. This type of flexing usually backfires. It makes it seem like we are not willing to be a team player. We just want to force our old ways onto our new team. Instead, listen to their ideas and routines. There will be plenty of time to share your ideas. They will be better received after you have built relationships through listening and understanding.

You can be the kind of teacher who loves to try new things in her classroom, wades through changes with ease, and looks at pretty stuff on the Internet without chasing someone else's idea of what success looks like. You can take in what the teacher next door is doing, review a brand-new curriculum dumped in your inbox a week before school starts, and open an app on your phone without feeling like you have to live up to an impossible standard.

I promise that's possible if you focus on being the best you. I couldn't be the best Sheri, but I could be the best Jamie. And my students loved me for it. I don't know about you, but trying new things in my classroom made me feel excited about showing up. When I chose projects that lit me up and made me feel joy, that was way more effective than something that was gorgeous and stressful. When I was finally able to stop comparing my classroom to classrooms I saw online and down the hall, I was able to focus on what was truly working and then, yes, make one change at a time to improve what wasn't.

· ·

If you have time to do only one thing from this chapter, I want you to:

Stop comparing yourself to other teachers.

I was never going to be Sheri. Hopefully I've made it abundantly clear that trying to do everything you see other teachers doing in their classroom is a recipe for disaster. You'll never be able to keep up, and even if you try really hard, that only leads to serious overwhelm and burnout. Resist!

· ·

The Not So Wimpy Way to Keep Your Eyes on Your Own Paper

1. Don't compare your backstage to their front stage (pages 156–158).

2. Don't compare your first act to their second act (pages 158–159).

3. Try one new thing at a time (pages 159–164).

4. Expect change (pages 164–167).

CHAPTER SEVEN

. . . .

Boundaries

hen my daughter Laynee was in kindergarten, her teacher had the whole class finish this sentence: "My mom loves to . . ."

Laynee wrote: "My mom loves to drink Mommy juice."

Meaning wine.

Luckily, her teacher thought it was hilarious.

As a teacher, you know that kids have zero boundaries.

Every K–4 teacher I know has learned the hard way not to wear open-toed shoes to school because kids can't resist tugging on toes during story time. Once when I was teaching, I was "gifted" a live scorpion. A Not So Wimpy team member, Kendra, used to get daily reports from a student on whether his dad had slept on the couch the night before. Kids will say and do the darndest things, as the saying goes, and get away with it because they are little and don't know any better. Adults could never behave the same way. (That's a good thing.) Adults need to have boundaries. *You* need to have boundaries.

Time out! Can we just stop and chat about the word "boundary"?

I used to hate this word. I thought of boundaries as rules I needed to follow. Boundaries made me feel like I was boxed in and had to behave the way that someone else had decided. Boundaries are why I couldn't wear jeans to school every day, why I had to use a specific curriculum even if it didn't work, and why I was required to attend a staff meeting every Friday afternoon when I was mentally exhausted.

At the time, I defined boundaries as something negative. I saw boundaries as arbitrary rules that were keeping me from doing what I really wanted and forcing me to do what someone else wanted. No wonder I never sat down and created any boundaries! Because within that definition, who would?

Funny enough, what I realize now was that the reason boundaries felt so negative to me was because I was living by boundaries that other people set. The reason I was annoyed was because I didn't have any boundaries of my own. Therefore, I didn't prioritize myself!

Boundaries are the limits we set for ourselves. Boundaries give us permission to say no to others. When you look at it this way, boundaries become so powerful!

I never knew that I had the right to set my own boundaries.

I thought a good teacher was always accessible and always said yes. I assumed that I needed someone else's permission to do otherwise. If you have ever felt that way too, let this be your permission slip to set some boundaries around what you'll agree to. It's been signed in all the appropriate places. You now have my permission to do less, say no, and prioritize your personal life. You can create healthy boundaries. You can't argue with a permission slip.

I actually don't have any authority to sign such a permission slip. The truth is that you never needed my permission, or anyone else's permission, for that matter. You've always had the right to set healthy boundaries. The reason so many of us don't set boundaries is because we don't know how to, and because our definition of success is based on the approval of other people. That's part of the reason we rewrote how you define success! (It's all starting to make sense now, isn't it?)

As teachers, we often don't set boundaries because "success" is tied to being the perfect teacher that we create in our head. (And think we see on Pinterest.) But here's the catch: chasing that version of success requires giving up all boundaries. That's not who you are anymore.

You have a new and better definition of success. (Head back to chapter 1 and re-read your definition if you haven't committed it to memory yet.) In order to achieve your new definition of success, boundaries are going to be as important as the secret stash of candy in your teacher desk drawer. In other words, boundaries are a must.

There are tons of different boundaries you might choose to create—in your classroom, at school, and everywhere else in your life. I'll get you started with a few that you should seriously consider adopting as you pursue your new definition of success as a teacher.

This is just a start, though, so feel free to put your thinking cap on and be as creative as a kindergartener with a box of crayons and a crisply painted white wall.

Boundary #1 • WORK HOURS

You can decide what your work hours will be. Obviously, there are some limitations. You are probably contracted for certain hours. Don't ignore your contract!! I don't want nasty notes from your principal.

Although you may not be able to declare your work hours to be 10:00 a.m. to

1:00 p.m. each day (that would be pretty cool), you can, and should, declare what your work hours will be outside your contracted hours. You do *not* need to work every night and all weekend. You are not at your students', your students' parents', or your administrators' beck and call. You can even decide not to work any additional hours beyond what your contract says. You get to decide!

Here are some questions to help you decide on your new work hours:

- What are your contracted hours?
- How many hours would you *like* to work each week? (You probably already made this decision when you wrote your definition of success.)
- How many of these hours would you like to work at school versus working at home?
- When you look at your personal/family calendar, which nights or days do you want to work less or not at all? (Hint: this can be every night if you choose!)

Now you are ready to decide on your specific work schedule. Grab your calendar and decide exactly when you will work each day of the week. Make certain that this new work schedule accurately reflects the number of hours in your definition of success.

When I first created my work schedule, it was my dream schedule. It wasn't a reality. I would go to work and things would pop up that did not fit into my ideal work schedule. There was an IEP meeting, a parent-conference night, or a school carnival. Honestly, this list could go on and on. There is always something extra we are asked to do. And I always said yes, because I didn't know any better. My work schedule was out the window almost every week. Writing down your dream schedule that you have no intention of enforcing is as good as buying a brand-new writing curriculum and never printing it. You can't benefit from this new boundary if you don't use it!

Here are some tips for enforcing your work schedule and making it a reality:

- Communicate your schedule to your spouse, family, friends, coworkers, administration, and class parents. You can post your work hours on your classroom door and in your email signature line. When people know your work hours, they won't be surprised when you have to say no.
- Practice saying no. It's not easy! When I was put on the spot, I almost always said yes. Take some time now to brainstorm some possible situations where you will be tempted to work outside of your work hours and write a response that values your new boundary. The more you prethink and practice how you will handle these situations, the easier it will be when the situation arises.

What to Say When You Want to Say No

When you inevitably get asked—or volunteered—to do something outside your work hours, here are a few responses.

"I am sorry. I am unavailable at that time. Will one of these alternate times work instead?"

"Unfortunately, I have a prior commitment and I will not be able to attend."

"In this season of my life, I am unable to volunteer for that activity."

After you communicate your nice no, celebrate, because sticking to your boundaries makes you an amazing teacher!

Boundary #2 • WORK EMAIL

If I really pushed your limits by suggesting that you set your own work hours, you better sit down for this one. It might just blow your mind. Are you ready? Here goes . . .

Don't check your work email during nonwork hours.

That means no checking your work email at night. It also means not checking your work email on the weekends. "But . . . but . . . Jamie, what if my principal sends me a super-important email over the weekend?" It's simple, really. The email will be there for you on Monday morning. It can wait. If it were truly an emergency, which it almost never is, your principal has your phone number and could give you a call.

I used to think there was really no harm in checking my work email at home. After all, I was already scrolling through social media and personal email on my phone. I would tell myself that reading a few work emails would help me get a head start and decrease my workload for the next day. I was totally lying to myself.

The reality is that nine times out of ten, the work emails would stress me out or make me think I needed to add extra tasks to my weekend to-do list. The emails stole my personal time. One time I received an email informing me that I would be getting a new student the following week. My relaxation time turned into stress. I madly started printing materials for the new student and called my best teaching buddy to complain about how unfair it was that I was getting the new student when my class was already so large. I spent the rest of the weekend preparing and feeling sorry for myself. I was tired when I got to school on Monday.

Another time I got an email from a parent on the weekend. They were furious about a grammar score their son had earned. The email was not kind in any way. I spent the rest of the weekend angry about the way that the parent had treated me. I went on and on to my husband about how the student was doing amazing overall but just struggled on the recent grammar quiz. They were still getting an A, for Pete's sake! I couldn't talk about or think about anything but the school situation. My weekend was ruined.

Checking your work email during nonwork hours will steal your personal time. Once you look, you will have a hard time not thinking about it. Often, you will become distracted from whatever you are doing or who you are with because you are trying to solve the problem in your head. Other times you will find yourself getting worried or upset about a situation. High achievers will even find themselves taking action. Maybe that means prepping a new activity, putting together a work packet for a student who will be absent, or reworking your lesson plans. It's hard to be present in your personal life when you let your work email move in on your personal time.

There is a country song by Sam Hunt called "Breaking Up Was Easy in the 90's." It makes me laugh because he sings about how in the nineties, there wasn't social media, so you didn't have to see what your ex was up to or whom they were with. It got me thinking that disconnecting and taking a break from work was probably easier in the nineties too. People didn't have easy access to their work from home. They didn't have cell phones with an email app. Heck, most homes didn't even have the Internet, and many didn't have computers. Technology has definitely made it more difficult for us to disconnect from work. Now we have to set more boundaries and be more intentional about leaving work at work.

One way to be more intentional with email is to decide when you will check it. You have already decided when you will not check email, right? *Right?* You're not checking email during nonwork hours.

So when will you check your email? You can't check it every moment of the school day. That would be distracting to your students. I know this for a fact. I had a terrible habit of leaving my email open on the classroom computer so that I could hear the little ding that indicated I had a new email. When the new email came in, I would casually stroll over to the computer to check out the subject line and decide if I wanted to open it immediately. I was doing all of this while trying to deliver high-quality lessons on fractions or central message.

And I'm not the only one.

For Valentine's Day one year, we wrote "I love you more than . . ." poems. Most students completed the sentence with words like tacos, candy, Legos, et cetera. But one of my little guys wrote, "I love you more than dicks." When I read it, my jaw dropped to the floor.

I was hoping that he had misspelled something that was a whole lot more appropriate.

I asked him to read it aloud to me.

"I love you more than dicks. You know? The sporting goods store!"

I was so relieved. I immediately helped him to capitalize and use an apostrophe.

I love to share this story each Valentine's Day with my online teacher community. We always get tons of replies. Most people want to tell us how funny it was and that they actually laughed out loud.

But every year we get a handful of emails from teachers who admit that their class read the subject line because the email showed up on their whiteboard . . . because they were checking email on the classroom computer like I used to. Oops!

And even if you aren't checking your email during your teaching time, you will need to be very careful that email does not interfere with your grading and lesson planning time. Email can really suck you in. It starts with the decision to check your email quickly before grading writing samples. Thirty minutes later, you realize you are still clicking around in your email and not one writing sample has been graded.

The solution? You might be catching on by now and know exactly what I am about to suggest. The solution is to put email on your calendar! Decide exactly when you will check email and how much time you will allow for email. Put the times on your calendar. I like to set aside thirty minutes per day for email. Since I am a morning person, I chose to schedule my thirty minutes of email time before school started each day. But you get to decide when it fits best in your schedule. Do you do it during your plan period? Is it the first thing you do after school or is it the last thing you do before going home? Whatever works for you, put it on the calendar.

You've now created some email boundaries! Congrats! That was the easy part. Now you must communicate and enforce these boundaries. Here are some tips to help you stay on track with your new boundaries.

- Take your work email app off your phone. Let your phone be a place for personal communication by removing the temptation to check those work emails from home. Seriously, do it right this moment. I'll wait.
- Decide on what your email turnaround time will be. Since you will not be answering your email immediately, how long can email wait for a response? If you are struggling with this one, start with a response time within twenty-four business hours. That means that if someone sends you

an email at five o'clock on Friday night, they can expect a response by five o'clock on Monday night. Put this turnaround time in your email signature so that everyone knows what to expect from you.

- Make the out-of-office email feature your very best friend. Sorry, chocolate! You've been replaced. Turning on an out-of-office notification each weekend is an easy way to communicate your boundary. If you receive an email over the weekend, the sender will automatically receive a response. It can be something like: "I am away from school over the weekend to spend more time with my family. Your message is very important to me and I will be certain to respond to you on Monday. Thank you!"

In this day and age, email is not the only way parents communicate with teachers. Many of you have some sort of classroom-management tool that includes communication similar to email or texts. There is nothing inherently wrong with using a tool like this. I am a huge fan of tools that make communication easier between school and home. However, we have to be careful about how we choose to use these tools. You are not always available to parents! In fact, all the boundaries and tips from above should still apply to your classroom-management tool.

- Do not answer messages during nonwork hours.
- Decide when you will respond to these messages and make sure the time is marked on your calendar.
- Remove the app from your phone if possible. At the very least, turn off the notifications.

The very greatest teachers cannot be reached 24/7. Instead, they are busy with family and hobbies in the evenings and on the weekends. This leads to a well-rested and super-interesting teacher on Monday morning who is fully present at school for their students. Counterintuitively, it also has a positive effect on parents: one Not So Wimpy Teacher, Kris, who stopped answering email after 4:00 p.m., swore to me that parents are happier when they don't hear from her.

Boundary #3 • FINDING YOUR POSITIVITY SQUAD

Student teaching for twelfth grade was a rude awakening for me. At the time, my own kids were very young, and the last time I had spent time with teenagers was when I was in high school myself. I was not prepared.

The first thing that I noticed was the language. As I listened to these students talk to each other, I couldn't help but wonder if they were having a contest to see who could fit the most swear words into one sentence. If that was the game, everyone was winning. I was taken by surprise when these teens didn't seem to know that you needed to speak differently to teachers than to friends.

But the biggest surprise of all is when I went to the restroom and saw something I will never be able to unsee. A couple was literally having sex in the hall. I kid you not. I was shocked, and when I went back to my classroom, I told my mentor teacher that kids had really changed since I was in high school. I knew he would understand because he was *my* teacher in high school.

But what he said surprised me. He said, "Kids haven't changed. The kids in your class swore and made bad decisions too. You just didn't notice because you didn't hang out with those kids. You were in a bubble."

I realized pretty quickly that he was right. The friends I spent my time with back in the day loved school, just like me. I guess I hung out with the nerds? Up until that moment, I had just assumed everyone behaved as well as we did in school. Apparently I was wrong.

My point is that the company you keep informs your perspective.

If your teacher friends are burned out and hate teaching, you will be in the same boat soon enough. If your friends work 24/7 and don't have any boundaries or practice self-care, you will probably do the same. But if you have friends who love connecting with their students, don't sweat the small stuff, and leave at their contracted time . . . well, there is a good chance you will follow in those footsteps too.

As teachers, every single one of us has had a tough day and gone to the staff room or our teacher bestie to complain. I think most teachers—and probably people in general—have a great desire to vent. Even though we have lots of work to do (and so do our coworkers), we can drop everything and start gossiping like it's the high school lunch table the week before prom. Seriously, everybody's done it. I like how it becomes a competition to see who has it the worst.

"You'll never believe the email his mom sent me today!"

"Oh, that's nothing! Listen to the email I got last week!"

We get a high from the venting and learn to enjoy commiserating with our coworkers. Before long, we spend nearly all our breaks with a group of complainers. Our habit of complaining with friends can become a bad habit super quickly. (More quickly than you might think). The most obvious downside to this habit is that you miss out on opportunities to get your work done. That twenty minutes spent complaining could be spent grading and allow you to go home on time with an empty bag. But the even more dangerous consequence is that we start sinking deeper and deeper into negative self-talk. We hear about everyone's terrible day and it's impossible to feel optimistic. We hear every complaint and it's hard to love our jobs.

Don't worry. I am not about to suggest that you never complain to your teacher bestie or that you completely ditch any person who is not positive 100 percent of the time. (You would probably be a pretty lonely person if you had to do that.) Instead, I want you to commit to seeking some balance. Teachers desperately need friends who understand the highs and lows of the classroom. But we also need friends who challenge and motivate us. We need friends who look for solutions rather than those who waste time with nothing but complaints. You need a positivity squad.

During my first year of teaching, I became great friends with the teacher next door, Jennifer. She was a very experienced teacher who was nearing retirement, but it was her first year at this particular school. I had several years of experience substituting at the school, but it was my first year as a teacher. We helped each other. Throughout the week we would meet and talk for hours about ways to help our students.

Jennifer was generally very positive, and when I was struggling, she would help me to brainstorm some solutions. (In fact, one of the very first Not So Wimpy Teacher resources was her idea!) Once per week we would go for happy hour. Over margaritas and flatbread pizzas, Jennifer would continue to share teaching lessons and encourage me after some super-tough days. And yes, during those happy hours we did complain a little. After all, we are human. I am certain those evenings are what got me through my first year of teaching. Jennifer helped me become a much better teacher for my students. She was my positivity squad.

Who is your positivity squad? It's easy to find a group of teachers to vent to, but it can be more challenging to find that person or those people who will lift your spirit and encourage your growth. You will probably have to seek out your positivity squad. Watch the way that people work and participate in team meetings. Your future positivity squad is probably seeking clarity and looking for solutions during these meetings rather than complaining and gossiping. Take note of the teachers who seem to find the joy or the lesson in difficult situations. When you hear them talking about what they will do differently next time, you know you have found your positivity squad. Look for other teachers who have healthy boundaries. Is there a teacher on your team who doesn't answer work emails on the weekend? I hope you find your positivity squad walking out to their cars right at their contracted time off! (Bonus points if they have an adorable bag that is *not* bulging with papers.)

If you are still struggling to find your positivity squad, do not despair. It can take time! In the meantime, start asking yourself if you are a positive coworker and teammate. When you exude the traits of a positivity squad, you are far more likely to attract your people. Here are some simple ways that you can start to bring some positivity to your relationships at school:

- Ask about their wins.
- Leave motivating notes.
- Surprise them with small gifts such as candy or coffee.
- Encourage them to stick to their boundaries by sharing your own journey.
- Ask for advice rather than venting.
- Give them this book to read!

In the meantime, feel free to join the Not So Wimpy Teacher Facebook groups. We are a huge community of teachers who seek to give ideas and help to problem-solve rather than vent. We would be happy to be your online positivity squad while you seek out an in-person squad.

I am not crazy. I know that your workplace is not all unicorns and rainbows. No matter how positive you are, you are going to have to work with people who moan, groan, and try to beat you down. Your teammates might prefer to complain about "kids these days" instead of researching new teaching strategies. Your team lead might drop by your classroom every morning to vent about late homework and ridiculous parent emails. Your principal might use every staff meeting to lecture about low test scores and new data-collection requirements. You aren't going to be able to change everyone's mindset. That is where the boundaries come in.

Decide now that you will intentionally spend more time with your positivity squad than the people who try to bring you down. For every minute you spend in a meeting with people complaining instead of problem-solving, schedule a happy hour or a planning session that is twice as long with your positivity squad. For every lunch break you spend listening to staff members vent and complain, spend twice as long celebrating wins with your best positivity-squad buddy.

Creating balance between the Negative Nellies and the Positive Patties will quickly help you to find that love for teaching again!

Boundary #4 • KNOWING WHEN IT IS TIME TO GO

Buckle up, because this is a deep one. In fact, for the longest time I didn't want to write about this in the book. Originally I was asked to write an entire chapter about it and I couldn't. I didn't want you to spend so much time reading about a negative topic. But after months of writing to you and feeling as though we have become teaching besties, I realize I would be doing you a disservice if I left the topic out completely. I am putting on my big-girl panties, because we need to have this conversation.

Not a day goes by that we don't have someone in our teacher Facebook groups post one of these questions.

"I'm thinking that I need to leave my school because it feels toxic. How do you know if it's time to look for a new job?"

"I don't think I can do it anymore. Is there anyone who has left the teaching profession? What other jobs are we qualified for?"

It's probably a good time to remind you of why I wrote this book. I most certainly did not want to write a book that would cause teachers to leave their profession. In fact, it is quite the opposite. I am passionate about keeping teachers in the classroom. My heart aches when I hear stats about how quickly teachers are leaving the profession. Colleges cannot train new teachers fast enough to replace the teachers who are leaving after only three years in the classroom. These are often individuals who decided they wanted to be teachers when they were small children. They are passionate about kids and desperate to make a difference. But as we all know, teaching can be all-consuming and thoroughly exhausting. I set out to write this book because I want to give all of you amazing teachers some tools to make teaching just a tad easier. I want you to find that childhood dream that you had. I want to help you rekindle that love. I want you to continue to teach.

But I want you to be happy, and the truth of the matter is that sometimes change is necessary. In order to fall back in love with teaching, you may need to leave your school and find one that is a better fit. And as much as I hate saying this, some of you may decide that teaching is not your true love and you may decide to explore a new career. You get to make the decision that is best for you. I support you 100 percent in whatever that decision might be.

Why I Left Teaching

I didn't leave the classroom because I stopped loving teaching. I wasn't burned out. In fact, I loved my position, my school, and the daily routines I had created. Even more, I loved my students and delivering engaging lessons every day. Sure, I hated staff meetings and boring professional-development activities. I had tough days when parents sent rude emails or students challenged me. But I knew I had found my calling and that, after several years of feeling like I was drowning, I was finally in a place where I could breathe.

So why leave? Two reasons:

First, I was having health problems. I suffer from epilepsy. I have seizures due to a brain injury. It is something I have struggled with my entire life, but it was not properly diagnosed until a couple years before I became a teacher. The reason it took so long to diagnose is that I rarely have grand mal seizures. Most of my seizures are staring seizures. They can be tough to spot, but they still leave me feeling off. My speech can be affected and my brain gets very foggy. If I have too many staring seizures in a short period of time, they will often lead to a grand mal seizure. Those act like a stroke. They take at least a month for me to recover from.

During my last year of teaching, I started to have seizures regularly. I would have them while I was teaching and while I was driving. There was no clear reason why the seizures were increasing, but I was starting to feel unsafe. I didn't feel like I should be driving myself to school or in charge of a room of twenty-five eight-year-olds who were depending on me. It made me so sad to think I could no longer do the job I loved due to my health.

The other reason I left was because of Not So Wimpy Teacher. I started my business as a hobby in 2013. I loved creating simple but engaging resources for my classroom. I thought that if I sold a few to other teachers, I could save them some time. I also thought that if I made about twenty dollars per month, I might be able to buy more resources, books, and manipulatives for my own students. I loved this new hobby so much that I would stay up late every night creating new sets of task cards and math centers. I created resources during family vacations and every single break from school. Teachers from all over the world were using my resources with their students! It was such an amazing feeling. I realized I may not be healthy enough to drive to school, but I am more than capable of sitting behind my computer and creating phenomenal resources for teachers and students. The kind of resources that make teachers and students love school.

So the short answer is, I left the classroom to protect my health and to make a massive impact in the world of education.

Changing schools or careers is definitely difficult, but often the decision to do so is actually the toughest part. Let's change that! Let's decide when you will leave before it even becomes an issue. We are deciding when you will quit before you've even seriously contemplated quitting.

This activity is especially powerful if you are happy at your school and not seriously looking for a new job. When we start thinking about quitting, it is generally because there is a lot of drama and feelings involved. There are usually specific incidents that make us angry or sad. That puts us in the position of trying to make a massive life decision when we aren't feeling our best. This can lead to poor decisions, feeling unsure about the decisions we've made, or being stuck unable to make a decision one way or the other. So, let's not wait until we feel so down-and-out to make this large, life-changing decision. Let's decide now.

Grab your flair pen and get comfy. I want you to take some time to brainstorm your answers to the statements below. Everyone's answers will be different and there are no right answers. You might have a long list or it might just be three or four items for each. The important thing is to take your time so that your answers are very specific. You might spend fifteen minutes on it now and then come back to it tomorrow when you've had even more time to reflect.

1. *I will leave a school when:*

2. *I will leave the teaching profession when:*

Remember that you can decide to leave for any one reason that you have listed or you can decide that you will leave if two or more of the items on your list become a reality. For some of you, maybe the entire list has to be true before you will leave. Set your boundary now!

If you are having trouble getting started with this exercise, you can use these examples as a starting point.

I will leave a school when:

- I am not allowed to make reasonable modifications to curriculum to best meet the needs of my individual students.
- my work-hour boundaries are not being respected at least 90 percent of the time.
- I feel as though my safety or the safety of my students is not being prioritized.

I will leave the teaching profession when:

- I no longer feel excited and motivated by student aha moments.
- even after implementing new strategies and boundaries, I find myself crying multiple times per month.
- my health deteriorates or is in jeopardy due to the stress or the work hours.

Taking time to decide when you would leave a job while you are actually happy or content with your job is powerful. Removing emotion from the decision allows you to make a choice that truly values you and your well-being. It's a lot like planning for the unexpected. There is something so freeing about knowing how you will handle situations before they even pop up!

COMMUNICATION IS KEY

You've done the hard work of deciding you deserve boundaries and then setting your first several limits. None of this will matter if no one knows about these boundaries. People cannot learn to respect your boundaries if they don't know that they exist. If you keep your work hours a secret, it's entirely possible that your principal will continue to schedule meetings during your personal time. If no one knows about your new email policy, you are likely to have parents and coworkers who complain that you didn't answer their question fast enough.

My doctor's office closes at 4:00 p.m. Inevitably I remember that I need to schedule an appointment at 4:05 p.m. It's annoying, but I know the hours, so I just set a timer to make the call in the morning. Their hours are communicated and so I respect them. I don't expect to call at 4:05 p.m. and have someone answer the phone.

Chick-fil-A is not open on Sundays. It's a huge bummer when you get a killer chicken sandwich craving on a Sunday afternoon. It's even more annoying when you actually forget that it is Sunday and drive to the restaurant only to find it dark and empty. It might not be convenient, but I know they are closed on Sundays. I don't have to love their hours, but the hours are communicated and so I respect them.

People will learn to respect your boundaries too if you communicate them. It might take time. They may still send emails on the weekend or interrupt your plan time just the way I have been known to drive to Chick-fil-A on a Sunday. They may not even like your boundaries. It drives me bonkers that I can buy only one package of toilet paper at Costco. Over time I am getting used to it and adjusting my shopping schedule to make it work. Your family, admin, students, and student families will also get used to your boundaries over time. They will adjust their habits to fit within your communicated boundaries.

Communicating your new limits can be very simple. Here are some ideas:

- Post your work hours on a sign near your classroom door, in your email signature, and in your classroom newsletter.
- Use out-of-office notifications to let coworkers and families know when they can expect an email response from you. If possible, do the same for any classroom communication or management tools.
- Use a sign on your classroom door to communicate to coworkers when you are planning or grading and should not be interrupted unless there is an emergency. (Include ways for people to contact you for nonemergency questions.)

Remember to overcommunicate. Don't be discouraged if you have to share your boundaries repeatedly. Since so few people have learned the importance of boundaries, it takes longer for us to train them to respect our limits. (Plus, people are forgetful!)

• •

If you have time to do only one thing from this chapter, I want you to:

Remove your work email from your phone and personal devices.

It's so simple, but it is the first step in creating intentional boundaries about email. You do not need to be available 24/7. I promise!

• •

The Not So Wimpy Way
to Set Boundaries

1. Choose and communicate your work hours (pages 173–175).

2. Set a boundary around work email (pages 176–181).

3. Find your positivity squad (pages 181–185).

4. Know when it is time to go (pages 185–190).

Optional:

* Practice saying no (pages 175–176).

CHAPTER EIGHT

· · · · · · · · · · · · · · · · ·

Not So Wimpy Wins

I tend to go overboard.

In fact, my husband says that the scariest thing ever is when I say, "I have an idea."

In 2022, while I was writing this book, all four of my teenagers went to prom. This will never happen again because my son was a senior. His graduation was only a month away and I was feeling so sentimental. Prom felt like the beginning of the end of high school. I handled it the only way that I know how: I went overboard on a huge prom celebration.

The prom venue was about an hour from our house. It was literally in the middle of nowhere. There were no nice (or even semi-nice) restaurants on the way or nearby. The idea hit me. I would transform my backyard into a beautiful, romantic restaurant for the kids, their friends, and their dates! I got giddy with excitement and then went crazy with planning the details.

I found a private chef, table rentals, a musician, and a photographer.

I picked out table settings and centerpieces that tastefully matched the school colors.

I put together a fancy menu that teenagers would actually enjoy.

I even rented a party bus to get the kids all the way to prom and back.

Absolutely everything was perfect.

The kids looked stunning in their gowns and tuxedos. My yard looked like a scene from a fairy-tale movie. The live music was fun and romantic. The photos are precious. I sure hope the kids loved it, because it is a night I will never forget. (And I didn't even get to wear a gown or go to the dance in the party bus!)

I don't know about you, but it's easy and so darn fun for me to celebrate family and loved ones. It's much more difficult for me to do nice things for myself.

If you're like me—and most teachers I know—you don't take much time to celebrate yourself. Think about it. When was the last time you treated yourself or celebrated a win? Simply taking the time to reflect on your accomplishments, your growth, and even the effort you put in every day as a teacher is so important to loving the work we do.

(Also, let me take a moment and say: yay you!)

In the early days of starting my business and teaching, I had no clue how to celebrate myself. At the end of each week, I felt exhausted and discouraged. I had a huge list of things that I didn't finish. I was hyper focused on the lesson that didn't go well. I was worried about the kiddo that seemed to be falling farther behind. I felt defeated because all I could see was the negative.

When I started my Not So Wimpy Teacher business, I began planning my schedule each week and blocking my time. This was especially important because

I was teaching full-time and running a small business on my own. I was definitely finishing tons of tasks, but at the end of the week I never felt accomplished. I was tired and overwhelmed by all of the things that I didn't finish.

Sound familiar?

That all changed when I met my life coach, Neill. I had no idea what a life coach was or that I needed one. The first time that I really talked to Neill was when we were sharing an Uber to the airport after attending a conference. She told me that she helped high achieving women become more productive and get the most important tasks completed in less time. I flat-out asked her, "Do I need a life coach?" The rest is history. After she helped me to tighten up the productivity in my personal and business life, she taught me about celebrating myself.

It was a foreign concept to me, as I am sure it is for you.

With some help from Neill, I realized I was not taking the time to celebrate my wins. I was finishing tasks and moving on to the next thing without even taking a moment to feel accomplished. And when something didn't go well during my week, I spent all kinds of time dwelling on it. I was giving the negative things that happened considerably more time in my day than anything positive. And I'm not alone.

Something Neill taught me is that it's actually our brain's *job* to solve problems—which is why our thoughts automatically skew to the negative. That's why it can be super easy to focus on the nasty parent email or the frustrating staff meeting instead of the kid who finally figured out how to subtract 6 from 10.

To prevent the black clouds in your day from obscuring the sun, you have to intentionally create time to celebrate your wins. If you don't create the space for wins, your brain will continue to hyper focus on the negative. There is nothing wrong with you. We are just human and this is how we are wired.

The process Neill taught me is simple.

Block out thirty minutes every Friday afternoon before heading home for the weekend. (If that feels forced or stressful, choose whatever time feels right for you.) I liked Fridays because I went home feeling proud and productive.

Put the time on your calendar so that it doesn't get forgotten. Honor this commitment to yourself. Do not allow yourself to replace this time with grading, lesson planning, or breakroom gossip. You deserve this time. If something pops up, love yourself enough to reschedule this date with yourself.

I suggest ordering a super-cute notebook and some scented flair pens (as you may have noticed, this is my solution for almost everything), but the notes app on your phone can do the trick as well. Do what feels good to you. Now comes the important part: get comfy and use the time each week to make a list of every single win from your week. Don't worry about handwriting, grammar, or complete sentences. (Has a teacher ever said those words before?) Your only focus is creating a list of things that went well during your week. These can be big wins or tiny baby wins. They all count.

Neill calls this list an accomplishment bank. Making a weekly deposit into this accomplishment bank will help you to focus on the dozens of ways that you are showing up as an amazing and effective teacher. The weekly deposits fill you with more confidence and joy. Your students, administration, and society *will* forget to tell you how unbelievable you are, but these regular deposits don't lie. This bank quickly starts to represent the very reasons that you love being a teacher.

I am always honest with you. (I am hoping that by this point we can be teacher besties.) So, I must warn you. At first it will be hard to think of a single win. You might think, "I had a terrible week. Nothing good happened." Or you might have trouble remembering anything from the beginning of the week. Sometimes those weeks can seem extra long. Am I right? Plus, your brain will try to tell you that a win is not good enough to write on your list. But push past these thoughts. Moments after these thoughts is when your brain is going to offer up the good stuff.

Don't quit before you get there. Instead, write down every single win that comes to your mind, no matter how small. (Small wins are the stepping stones to the huge wins!)

If you are struggling to remember wins from earlier in the week, you might want to spend five minutes at the end of every day jotting down the wins. This might be the perfect system for you!

And remember: no one else will ever see this list. It's just for you! It's like your secret diary. You can be as cheesy as you want. I won't tell.

IF YOU FEEL LIKE YOU DON'T HAVE ANY WINS . . .

You are normal! I went through the same thing when I started my accomplishment bank.

In my teacher Facebook groups, I often ask teachers to share a win from their week. I am sad but not surprised that these posts generally get fewer responses than all my other posts. I might have a few teachers who share a win, but they are quick to call their win "small" or "silly."

However, the most common comment I get on my win posts is something like, "I survived." While I enjoy embarrassing my teenagers by loudly belting out, "At first I was afraid, I was petrified," the truth is that I am scared for you if the only win you had all week was staying alive. I am going to call your bluff here. I am 99.9 percent certain that you had a plethora of other wins during the week—even if you had a seemingly tough week. You are just having trouble focusing on them because of those pesky negative thoughts. It's so easy for teachers—or anyone really—to get bogged down in negativity because our brain prioritizes it.

The good news is that when you get in a routine of recognizing and celebrating your wins, it will gradually become easier and easier. Your brain can be trained to see those wins and point them out to you the same way that it currently points out all of the things that aren't going well. In the meantime, I want to give you lots of categories of wins.

Use these ideas as starting points. You might have a win that does not fit in any of these categories, and that's not a problem. But use this list anytime you feel like you don't have a single win to write on your list. Use it when you are feeling extra exhausted and can't find the energy to come up with your wins from scratch.

And definitely use it when the only win your brain is offering up is that you aren't dead.

Student relationships

Relationships are the heart and soul of teaching. There is no strategy more important than creating trusting and open relationships with your students. They won't learn from you if they don't think you like them. Let's not forget to look for and celebrate these wins.

- Did you have a conversation with a student that helped you to get to know them on a more personal level?
- Did you check in with a student you have been worried about?
- Did you take time to learn something new about a student's culture, language, religion, or beliefs?
- Did you have a student that trusted you enough to come to you to talk about a situation happening at home or at school?

- Did you have a class meeting to connect with your students and address a situation in the classroom?
- Did you ask your positivity squad for suggestions about how to help or connect with a student?
- Did you help a set of students to reconcile their differences?
- Did you teach a lesson about diversity and inclusion?
- Did you teach a lesson about friendship?
- Did you provide opportunities for students to practice working together with teammates or a small group?
- Did you send home a happy note or make a happy call to a student's guardian?

Student success

Sure, we all get excited when the entire class does well on the math-unit test. And we should! That's a win for certain. But don't forget that student success is not all tied to grades. Therefore, teacher success is not all tied to grades either!

You wrote your definition of success and I bet it's so much more than testing scores. Always be on the lookout for signs of success that the gradebook won't necessarily show. Don't be scared to write student successes on your list of wins. You have provided the lessons, the opportunities, and the environment that has contributed to this success. Every student win is your win too!

- Did you have a student who had an aha moment during a lesson?
- Did you have a student who attempted something challenging and above level?

- Did you have a student who asked you for help even though they are generally too nervous to do so?
- Did you have a student who helped another student with a skill or assignment?
- Did you have a student who asked a great discussion question?
- Did you have an effective small-group lesson where students seemed to make progress towards their goals?
- Did you have a student who successfully completed test corrections?
- Did your students finish a large project?
- Did you have a student who felt proud of themselves?

Your lessons

Teachers put so much thought and creativity into their lessons. You are always looking for ways to make your lessons more engaging, inclusive, and effective for all students. Don't forget to celebrate these wins!

- Did you try something new this week?
- Did you simplify a lesson or procedure in your classroom?
- Did you get your students up and moving?
- Did you notice that a lesson wasn't connecting and then make on-the-spot changes to get back on track?
- Did you allow for student choice this week in one of your lessons?
- Did you have fun teaching a lesson or activity?
- Did your students have fun completing a lesson or activity?

Productivity

Remember that productivity isn't getting every item checked off the to-do list. That will never happen! Instead we are focusing on finishing the most important tasks during our scheduled work hours.

- Did you plan your nonteaching time for the week?
- Did you complete your next batch of lesson plans?
- Did you complete any grading?
- Did you delegate any of the tasks on your to-do list?
- Did you delay or delete any of the items on your to-do list?
- Did you say no to something that did not fit on your calendar?
- Did you use your plan time to finish tasks?

Work and life balance

The only way you can really truly love teaching is if you have some balance between your work and your personal life. Don't listen to the naysayers who say that it isn't possible to have balance. You have an entire book filled with tools to simplify teaching so that you can enjoy more nonwork time. Don't forget to celebrate yourself when you begin using these strategies!

- Did you leave one day at your contracted time?
- Did you stick to your decided work hours all week?
- Did you spend time with your positivity squad?
- Did you avoid checking your school email from home? (If not, did you do better than last week?)

- Did you avoid lesson planning and grading from home? (If not, did you do better than last week?)
- Did you spend extra time with the people or hobbies that you love?

One very important thing I want you to notice about these wins is that the majority of them are within your control. You aren't waiting for standardized test scores or a thank-you email from a parent or an administrator. I encourage you to celebrate those wins if and when they happen, but I want you to see that there are tons of wins that you achieve every week. Your wins are about the effort you are putting in rather than what others notice. These are your confetti moments! You create these moments and you get to celebrate them.

Not So Wimpy Weekly Wins

Even though I am no longer in the classroom, I still celebrate wins every week as the CEO of Not So Wimpy Teacher. Celebrating the wins every week helps remind me of the impact we are making. If I didn't take time to recognize the wins it would be easy to look right past the great things we are doing in the world of education and instead focus on the things that didn't go well or the projects we haven't finished.

I still use a similar procedure for wins. The biggest difference is that I share my wins. You certainly do not have to. Every Friday afternoon I sit down with my phone and I brain dump all of the things that myself and my team have made progress on during the week. I record all the lessons we got to learn and all the times we worked hard. I copy all these wins into our company communication app. I am sure to tag any team members that worked on the projects or in some way contributed to the win. No matter how boring or tough our week was, I am always able to come up with at least a dozen wins to share with my team.

After I share the wins, I encourage my team to add any additional wins I might have missed or not known about. I encourage them to call out any team member that helped them during the week.

My whole team looks forward to the Not So Wimpy Weekly Wins, but they probably don't even realize I do it every week for me. No matter how long I have been doing this, I need the reminder that my work matters and that I am making a difference. We all need that reminder, and we can't wait for someone else to tell us.

CELEBRATING YOUR WINS

Simply taking time to recognize your wins is a celebration in and of itself. It gives you a sense of accomplishment and puts a smile on your face. I know that writing out my wins always sends me into the weekend feeling proud and even excited for the following week. Sometimes this is enough of a celebration.

Other times I really want to reward myself. If that is you, lean into it. You earned it! When we celebrate wins, we are more likely to keep working toward that definition of success. We are more likely to protect our boundaries and prioritize the tasks that matter. After all, your brain loves to celebrate and to be rewarded. It wants to feel that pleasure again.

When Neill suggested that I start planning some celebrations for specific wins, I was embarrassed to admit that I had no clue how to celebrate myself. I had lost track of all hobbies and I had been so busy that I couldn't even remember the last time that I had done something for myself. Sound familiar? Don't feel guilty. The more you ask your brain how you can celebrate your achievements, the more it will start to offer up those amazing ideas. Don't put pressure on yourself to come up with an over-the-top Hollywood-glam-worthy celebration. The simple things are usually the best anyway! Here are a few ideas to get your brainstorming started:

- Happy hour with your spouse or a friend
- A manicure or a pedicure (at home or at your favorite nail salon)
- Take out for dinner
- Breakfast in bed
- A hike or a bike ride on your favorite trail
- A lazy afternoon browsing at your favorite bookstore
- A day spent in your pajamas
- An afternoon enjoying your favorite craft

Don't feel guilty about indulging in yourself. You earned every moment. Take the time to pat yourself on the back.

CELEBRATING STUDENT WINS

I wish I had learned how to celebrate my own wins at a much younger age. If someone had taught me the importance of recognizing my own wins when I was a child, I would have a much better built-in habit as an adult. Instead I was the type of student who would finish a research paper and barely breathe a sigh of relief before starting on the next project. Every day was just a series of tasks I had to complete. If I completed them, I was on track, and if I didn't complete a task, then I was behind. I took no joy in my success. I didn't even notice it.

Now that you are learning the importance of celebrating our own wins, you have the special opportunity of teaching this habit to your students. They can learn from a young age to look for the small wins and not to wait for someone else to toot their horn. Teach them to take pride in their accomplishments.

The procedure I used in my classroom was very similar to my personal win procedure. Every student had a Friday Journal. This can be a spiral or composition notebook. You can even make do with pronged folders and loose-leaf paper. The last ten minutes of every Friday were dedicated to writing in our journals. This had nothing to do with writing workshop. It was not a graded assignment. Instead, students wrote a letter to their adult to tell them about their wins during the week. They could write in sentences or make a list. The format didn't matter. The important part of the exercise was to dig deep and take note of the amazing new things they had accomplished or learned during the week. Sometimes I would help them brainstorm by writing on the board some lessons or activities that we had completed that week. Or I might write some questions to get them thinking.

- Did you complete an assignment this week that you were proud of?
- Did you learn something new?
- Did you practice something that has been challenging for you?
- Did you help a classmate or a friend?
- Did you raise your hand and participate in a lesson?
- Did you write or read about something that was especially interesting?

Students would bring their notebooks home over the weekend. They were encouraged to share the note or list with their adult, but it was not required. (Remember that some people like to keep their win journal private.) Some adults would write a letter back in the notebook. I talked to my class about the fact that adults are very busy and every adult won't have time to write a note. It was not required. It was not their homework assignment. I never had a student who was disappointed by not receiving a note back. But if I did, I was prepared to write a short note to that student every few weeks.

I loved how much my students started looking forward to writing in their Friday Journal. They were so proud of their weekly letters. At the end of the year, when we were making memory books, many of my students chose to write about how much they loved their Friday journal time. This one simple activity helped my students recognize their growth. They learned to be proud of their work. And all it took was a notebook and ten minutes of class time!

If you have time to do only one thing from this chapter, I want you to:

Start an accomplishment bank.

Recognizing wins each and every week becomes a catalyst for continued success in the classroom. Our brain loves to tell us when we aren't good enough. It's time to remind your brain how incredibly amazing you really are. Set aside fifteen to thirty minutes every Friday to list out every big and small accomplishment from the week. Make this a date with yourself that you don't break.

The Not So Wimpy Way to Celebrate Your Wins

1. Choose a time once a week to record your wins (pages 198–204).

2. Teach your students how to celebrate wins (pages 207–208).

3. Choose some activities that you'll do to celebrate (page 206).

. . . .

CHAPTER NINE

Your End-of-Unit Assignment

T was the night before Christmas and all through the Searses' house the floors were covered in sparkling cider and millions of shards of glass.

I had the house professionally cleaned before a holiday dinner. My daughters Danika and Makenzie spent at least an hour setting and decorating the dinner table. We carefully picked out the perfect tablecloths and napkins. We added wine glasses at every seat to be used for our sparkling cider toast. The end product was gorgeous. I took tons of pictures as proof.

Soon my family arrived, the carols were playing, and the homemade pastas were ready. We all started to fill our plates with yummy foods. And then it all collapsed. Literally. The entire table collapsed. Wine glasses full of sparkling cider crashed to the floor sending glass shards from the kitchen to the living room. Plates of food, candles, and the butter dish fell to the floor. My clean house was a huge sticky mess. I had spent so much time worrying about how clean the house was and how pretty the table looked, but I had failed to secure the foundation—the table.

When it comes to teaching, most of us (it is not just you) are guilty of spending a ton of time on outward appearances and losing sight of the foundations. We are decorating our classrooms with a cute theme, labeling all the things, hanging artwork in the hallway, and wearing our cute teacher T-shirts. It looks good, just like my Christmas Eve dinner table. But we haven't created systems, declared boundaries, or learned to recognize our worth outside test scores. If we don't make some changes, the table is going to collapse. We will completely lose sight of our love for teaching.

What happens when you teach a lesson and give your students oodles of different strategies? If they are anything like my students were (and I am guessing they are), they will get overwhelmed and do nothing. When a lesson is too meaty, students get lost. They don't know where to start. That's why you (being the amazing teacher that you are) break down your lessons into small pieces and help your students to take one step at a time.

If you have read through the entire book, then you know I have given you oodles of tools that are meant to build a solid foundation. Oodles of tools in one book can feel like a maxi lesson in your classroom where no one knows where to start. But you have me, and I would not leave you stranded. I am going to break down the lessons from this book into twenty-one baby steps for you. By doing one small thing each day, you will be drastically changing the way you feel about teaching. In just twenty-one days, you will be madly in love with your chosen career. Are you up for the challenge?

Keeping Your Promises to Yourself

My coach, Neill Williams—the lady I shared an Uber with in the last chapter—talks a lot about keeping the promises we make to ourselves. It's one of the hardest things we can do as teachers because we're basically trained to do the opposite.

I asked her to contribute her advice on how to maintain all the amazing changes you've made by reading this book and continue to love teaching. Here's what she said.

"Keeping your promises to yourself is the skill of all skills. This will be what determines whether or not you can create new habits, and whether your future will be a recycled version of your past or you live the life of your dreams.

"Keeping your promises to yourself is not something you are born with. It's a skill that must be developed. But that's the best news. Since it's a skill that means you can create this for yourself, no matter who you are or what you have or haven't followed through on in your past.

"The message we receive from society is that we should prioritize our time, energy, and efforts toward other people. Many of us feel guilty at the mere thought of doing something for ourselves over doing something for someone else. By doing that, not only do we train ourselves to break our promises to ourselves, but we can get to a place where we don't even know what we want anymore because we have ignored our own inner knowing for so long.

> "When you say yes to yourself and truly master the skill of keeping your promises to yourself, you can do anything. The habits you create from keeping your promises to yourself won't be the ones that you do for a few weeks or months and then give up on.
>
> "These habits are meant to stick."

In order to make sure that you don't lose sight of your desire to fall back in love with teaching, I'd love to send you a quick message each day with your challenge reminder. I promise that the messages will be super short and sweet. No stories about eating fish, poopy rugs, or biting dental hygienists. These messages will just send your daily step in the twenty-one day challenge and encourage you to take that step. You can just think of me as another member of your positivity squad. Visit notsowimpyteacher.com /bookresources to join in on the fun.

Your success is so incredibly important to me. It is the very reason that I wrote this book. I have listed twenty-one small steps that are going to make a massive difference in your life. Use this chapter as a checklist for the next three weeks. Make a promise to yourself that you will execute one step a day. You can put the book somewhere where you will see it every day. But if you are anything like me, you will forget after a few days. You will fall back into your unhealthy routines. (It's the very reason that I never succeed at my yearly weight loss resolution.)

So here is your end-of-book assignment.

You don't have to use complete sentences.

Handwriting and spelling do not count.

Your assignment is due in twenty-one days, but I accept late work. Sound good?

Day 1 • WRITE DOWN YOUR NEW DEFINITION OF SUCCESS.

Have you written your definition yet?

Maybe you thought it was too woo-woo and so you skipped that section. Maybe you were skimming and missed that section. Or maybe your scented flair pen ran out of ink and you forgot to come back to it. Whatever the reason, the good news is that it is not too late. You'll still get full credit for this assignment.

If you do nothing else in this challenge (which would be crazy), do this.

Up until this point, it's likely that you have been defining success with someone else's definition. This could include getting high test scores, having cute bulletin boards and creating elaborate lessons. Frankly, this old definition sucks the fun out of teaching. Success is very personal. And that means the definition of success must also be personal. Every teacher has to decide on their own definition of success. When you have a clear vision of what it means for you to be a good teacher, you will know exactly which strategies need to be implemented right this moment and which ones can wait.

Head to page 35 to write your definition of success using a simple fill-in-the-blank template.

Day 2 • DECIDE WHICH PLANNER YOU ARE GOING TO USE.

Today is a fun day! All you have to do is pick your planner (and order it if necessary).

I am not talking about a lesson planner. I am talking about a calendar you can use to plan out your nonteaching time. You will use this planner to document the exact times that you will complete specific tasks. This calendar will help you to track exactly when you are going to grade tests, batch lesson plans, and check your email.

I am often asked for planner recommendations. Everyone is so different and it's important that you pick a planner that works for you. My best recommendation is to keep it simple. When something is simple, you are more likely to keep up with it. So I would probably ditch the bullet journal (unless you are certain that is the planner that speaks to you). Remember that using a simple Google calendar is perfectly fine! If you prefer a paper planner (I am a paper planner girl for sure!) I would suggest looking for a planner that includes hourly time slots for each day. This will make it easier to give each of your tasks a very specific time. If you want more guidance on what planner to look for, check out pages 40–42.

Day 3 • SET YOUR WORK HOURS.

I know you just got a new planner, but put your pens and stickers down! Before you go writing in your new planner, you need to decide on the hours you are going to work each week. If you don't decide on your work hours, you will end up overworking. You probably have contracted hours that you are required to work, but beyond that, you get to decide when you will work. Yep, you get to decide!

Head to page 29 for some tips to help you decide on your ideal schedule.

Day 4 • BRAIN DUMP AND CLASSIFY.

Too often we burden our brain by asking it to remember everything that we need to do. Other times, we create multiple lists that we don't stand a chance at completing.

Both strategies leave us feeling disappointed when we don't get everything done. But the reality is that we don't need to get everything done! We just need to get the most important tasks done. That's it!

Schedule some time today to do a full brain dump of everything you think you need to do. Include personal and professional tasks. Don't get overwhelmed by the size of the list. You are *not* going to complete it all this week. After you have created this large list, start to classify each item on the list as important, delay, delegate, or delete.

Head to page 49 for more details about doing your brain dump and using the Triple D strategy.

Day 5 • SCHEDULE TO FINISH.

Grab those pens because today is the day that you get to start writing in that beautiful planner that you picked. (Or maybe you are typing on your Google calendar. That's cool too!) You'll also need that list of important tasks that you created yesterday. It's time to break down each task and schedule a time (during your work hours) to complete the task. The key is that the task must be small enough that you can complete it during the time that you chose. We are not just "working on grading."

We are "grading five reading response essays." If you are working on grading and you finish only five essays, you feel unproductive and stressed. If you decide to finish grading five essays and you complete that small task, you feel like a superhero.

Head to page 47 for more tips about creating your ideal schedule.

Day 6 • PACE YOURSELF.

Sure, we have a list of standards that must be taught (and hopefully mastered). But how will you make sure there is enough time to fit each of these standards into your lesson plans? You know the destination, but now you need a map so that you know how to get there. A pacing guide is your map of lessons for the year. If you already have a pacing guide for each subject that you teach, you can pat yourself on the back and cash in on that "no homework" pass today. If you do not have a quality pacing guide, today is the day that you are going to make it happen.

You can go back to page 61 for directions for creating your own pacing guide. Or you can cheat. (Yup, the teacher is giving you permission to cheat!) Why start from scratch if someone has already done the work for you? Let's find a done-for-you pacing guide.

I have created pacing guides for grades two to five that you can grab for free. (Check out notsowimpyteacher.com/bookresources for all the freebies!)

Ask your grade-level team if they have created a pacing guide.

Join a Facebook group for your grade level and ask in the group if anyone has created a pacing guide that they would be willing to share.

Day 7 • BATCH.

Batching similar tasks is a super simple way to be productive while freeing up time in your busy schedule. Instead of lesson planning for every subject each week, you can speed up the process by focusing on multiple weeks of plans for just one subject. There are two different strategies that you can use for batching your lesson plans. You can either plan five weeks of one subject each week or plan a complete unit for one subject each week. Planning five weeks of lessons every week will be easier to track on your calendar. Planning for an entire unit will require more intention when scheduling, but can save even more time in the long run. Either way, they are both effective strategies.

Decide which batching plan is best for your personality and your current season of life. (Know that this decision is not written in stone, so don't overthink it.) Go back to pages 66–68 for more clarification about the batching types and example schedules.

After you have decided on your batching type, put time to do your first batch of lessons on your calendar.

Don't you just love two-part homework assignments?

Day 8 • MAKE ROUTINES YOUR FRIEND.

Daily and weekly routines are going to make lesson planning so much easier and quicker. When every Monday looks the same each week, you know exactly what you need to prepare every week. You will spend significantly less time looking for new ideas.

Choose *one* subject and decide on the daily and/or weekly routine that you will implement within the next two weeks. Make sure to flip back to page 74 for some examples of time-saving daily and weekly routines for different subjects.

Day 9 • GO BACK TO THE BASICS.

All too often we rush through teaching classroom procedures, like what to do when a student needs to use the bathroom or wants to read a book that's in your library. Perhaps you feel pressure to jump right into your pacing guide and teaching all the things before standardized tests are scheduled.

Or, if you are anything like me, you might not have even realized there were so many procedures that need to be taught. Either way, when we rush these lessons, we set ourselves up for major frustration all year. And, as many of us unfortunately know, it's hard to love teaching when your class feels out of control.

Start by identifying which subject or part of the day seems the most unruly in your classroom. Make a list of the procedures, rules, and routines that you want students to implement during that particular time. Add these lessons to your plans for sometime during the next week.

And if you are reading this during the summer—you're not off the hook.

Plan now to spend more time on procedures than usual when school starts.

Flip to page 95 for some fun and simple ways to teach or review routines and procedures. You'll also find a list of procedures you should consider teaching in your classroom on our book resources page at notsowimpyteacher.com /bookresources.

Day 10 • AUDIT YOUR SYSTEMS.

Quality systems make the regular tasks in your classroom easier and faster. If our systems are convoluted and outdated, they might be causing you extra stress and time. Take some time today to audit your classroom systems for restroom breaks, pencils, behavior, and classroom jobs. Here are some questions to ask yourself:

Do I have an established system for this particular task?

Is this system so simple that my students can manage it with minimal help from me?

How much classroom time is this system currently taking each day/week?

What can be done to simplify the system?

Make sure you head to page 98 for some examples of simplified systems that I used in my classroom.

Day 11 • MAKE SMALL GROUPS AND CENTERS EASIER TO MANAGE.

Small group is the time when you get the most aha moments from students because you are able to provide differentiated support. Aha moments are one of the most nourishing parts of the job and certainly help to keep the love alive. The problem is that we have been taught to make centers and small-group time complicated. We meet with too many groups each day, use center activities that are hard to prepare, and make unnecessarily complicated lesson plans for our groups.

Take some time today to audit your routine for centers and small-group time.

What is one change that you can make that will simplify this time in your classroom?

If you need some ideas, be sure to flip to page 102.

Day 12 • PLAY FAVORITES.

You might not be allowed to have a favorite student, but you most certainly can have a favorite subject. What subject do you love to teach the most? Why do you think you are good at teaching that subject? What strategies do you use to help your students to be successful? Make a list!

Now, what is your least favorite subject to teach? Take a look at your list of strategies and circle ones that could be used with your least favorite subject. You might be surprised by how often something that works well in one subject will work just as well in another.

Check out page 113 for an example of how I created this list and used it to help me to fall in love with teaching writing.

Day 13 • MAKE IT FUN.

Let's be clear: you are *not* a clown at a birthday party. Your job is not to entertain your students. That being said, teaching is more fun when our students are having fun. The key is to keep it simple so that you aren't too tired and overwhelmed to enjoy seeing your students enjoying themselves. Going all out is fine every once in a while, but simple is more sustainable over time.

Go back to page 114 for some easy ideas to add fun to your lessons.

Choose just *one* and add it to your lesson plans for sometime in the next two weeks. Remember that we are taking baby steps rather than adding lots of new things to your plate at one time.

Day 14 • GRADE LESS.

Repeat after me, "I do not need to grade every assignment my students complete." Say it again! Keep saying it until you believe it. Students do not complete assignments to get a grade. Oftentimes, assignments are just practice. We don't want to take a grade until students are ready to show what they know.

Today's task is to do an audit of the assignments that you are regularly grading each week. Which assignments can you stop grading? Which assignments are just for practice or do not accurately and fairly show what your students know? Decide not to grade these assignments going forward.

If you need some help recognizing things that no longer need to be graded, flip back to page 127.

Day 15 • KEEP IT INFORMAL.

Informal assessments are the key to knowing how your students are progressing toward mastery without having to take a stack of papers home to grade. In just a matter of minutes you will know who needs extra support or a reteach lesson. Informal assessments can become a regular part of your classroom routine and culture.

Choose one type of informal assessment to implement in your classroom within the next week. Need some ideas? Head to page 129 for a list of possibilities.

Day 16 • PUT IT ON THE CALENDAR.

Being intentional about when you grade can help to prevent Sunday-night scaries. You know the feeling . . . when you realize that your bag full of papers never left your car all weekend? Yep, that.

Instead, decide to get grading done during your chosen work hours. The best way to be successful is to break down your grading into small tasks, and schedule on your calendar exactly when you will complete each of those small tasks. Instead of setting time aside to "work on grading math tests," you might instead schedule time to "finish grading five math tests."

Put your grading on the calendar for the next week.

Check out page 145 for more tips on scheduling your grading time.

Day 17 • ASK FOR HELP.

The most successful people ask for help. For example, a professional football player needs the help of teammates, coaches, medical staff, and trainers. They are incredibly talented, but even they can't do their job alone. And, it feels so darn good to get to help someone. Give people this opportunity in your classroom!

If you are allowed (and don't just assume that you are not allowed), ask parents if they would be willing to volunteer in the classroom for a couple of hours every week or every other week.

There are lots of ways that families can help in your classroom even though they don't have education degrees. Check out page 142 for some ideas that can save you so much time.

Day 18 • SET YOUR BOUNDARIES.

Boundaries give you permission to say no, and today we are saying no to answering work emails 24/7. Looking at emails during your personal time can easily steal your joy and your time. You do not need to be on call. It is perfectly acceptable and professional to return emails within twenty-four business hours of receiving them.

This is a two-part assignment. You need to complete both parts in order to receive full credit.

Take your work email off your phone.

Set up an email out-of-office message that you will turn on when you leave school on Friday afternoons. It can say something like, "I am away from school over the weekend to spend more time with my family. Your message is very important to me and I will be certain to respond to you on Monday. Thank you!" And if you want some help learning how to set boundaries, check out pages 173–186.

Day 19 • JOIN OUR SQUAD.

Every teacher needs a positivity squad. We need people who motivate us and encourage us to stick to our boundaries. I hope that you have at least one person at your school who can be your squad. (Need a reminder on who gets to be in your positivity squad? Check out pages 181–185.)

Either way, I have created a huge community of incredible teachers. We would love to have you join our squad. You'll have instant access to tens of thousands of teachers who share ideas, resources, and words of encouragement. We don't have to do this alone!

Join one of our grade level Facebook groups. It's easy to find us online. Just search for "Not So Wimpy Teachers" and you'll find a bunch of different groups for each grade level.

Day 20 • CELEBRATE GOOD TIMES!

You are a phenomenal teacher. You have so many small and huge wins every single week. It's time to give yourself permission to celebrate all of those moments. Celebrating can be as simple as recognizing your wins.

Take time today (or schedule it for Friday afternoon) to brainstorm all of your wins from this week. If you need some help getting started, check out page 205. We have listed several different examples of wins that are sure to get your win flowing.

Day 21 • SPREAD THE GOOD NEWS.

I hope that this book has given you plenty of new strategies and a healthier mindset about your job as a teacher. Even more, I hope that implementing these strategies has you falling in love with teaching all over again. I want this for every teacher!

Your last assignment is to share this book with a teacher friend.

You can help another teacher fall madly and deeply in love with teaching!

FROM ME TO YOU

Honestly, writing this book was not easy. (I now have such respect for all book authors!) There were numerous times that I wanted to quit. I wrote through two pregnancies, nonstop morning sickness, and two miscarriages. It would have been easy to put this dream off until life was easier. No one would have known the difference.

Except I would.

I know how much this book is needed.

I know that incredible, compassionate, and talented teachers are leaving the classroom in droves. Even more teachers are staying, but they are burned out and quickly losing their love for teaching. It's not sustainable. The book could not wait. *You* could not wait.

I am proud of you for pushing through and making it to the end of this book. I know that you are very busy and that your time is incredibly valuable. Now that you are the kind of person who celebrates your own wins, make sure you list reading this book to the end as a win. And if you completed the twenty-one-day assignment, you have most certainly earned a special reward from yourself. You've earned an A+ from me! Your success is inevitable.

May you never forget that you are *not* a wimpy teacher and may you always be madly in love with teaching.

ACKNOWLEDGMENTS

. . . .

Once upon a time there was a young girl who dreamed of writing a book. She spent school recesses reading a thesaurus and adding "interesting" words to her stories. (Clearly, she wasn't too popular with the other third graders). This wannabe writer even sent countless letters to her favorite author, Ann M. Martin, asking how to become a published writer.

That young girl was me! And thirty-plus years later, I actually wrote and published a book! But I certainly did not achieve this bucket list dream by myself.

Thank you Scott for always encouraging and allowing me to pursue my crazy ideas. You've always been my biggest fan and the first person to ask for my autograph.

Thank you Kyler, Danika, Makenzie, Laynee, Adalynn, and Hazel for letting me share so many stories about you throughout the book (even though I didn't give you a choice). I truly hope that I was able to be a great teacher *and* a great mom because you deserve the very best.

Thank you to the Not So Wimpy Teacher team: Beth, Lindsay, Diana, Lisa,

Katie, Mary, Kendra, and Irene. You are all unicorns who make magic happen every single day. Plus, I am eternally thankful that you put up with my countless *Big Bang Theory* references.

Thank you to my business coach, Rick Mulready. I love that you serve tacos at all of your retreats, and I'm thankful for everything you've done to help me make a massive impact in the world of education. Thank you to my life coach, Neill Williams. I had no idea that I needed a life coach until I met you. Now, I wonder how I ever made it without you.

Thank you to my collaborator, Meghan Stevenson. Laughing at our weekly meetings will be my fondest memory from writing this book! But seriously, you made my words sound so much better. I didn't even need the thesaurus. Every author needs a Meghan.

Thank you to my agent, Steve Troha. You stepped in and saved the day.

Thank you to everyone at Portfolio and Penguin Random House for making this huge Google doc into an actual book, including Veronica Velasco, Helen Healey, Carlynn Chironna, Madeline Rohlin, Megan Gerrity, Meighan Cavanaugh, Mary Kate Skehan, Jacquelyn Galindo, Lauren Monahan, Savana Bishop, Margot Stamas, Stefanie Brody, Sarah Brody, Brian Lemus, Andrew Lau, Naomi Cho, Jen Heuer, Emilie Mills, Anna Scheithauer, Jessica Regione, Bria Sandford, Niki Papadopoulos, and Adrian Zackheim.